The Perfect Patchwork Primer

The Perfect Patchwork Primer

By Beth Gutcheon

*illustrated by Barbara Stockwell
and Jeffrey Gutcheon*

photographs by Bevan Davies

**David McKay Company, Inc.
New York**

The Perfect Patchwork Primer

LIBRARY OF CONGRESS CATALOG CARD NUMBER: 73-76563
MANUFACTURED IN THE UNITED STATES OF AMERICA
ISBN: 0-679-50385-4

Fourth Printing, July 1974

To Jeffrey and David
For Whom, and Without Whom

With thanks to the Shelburne Museum, to Eleanor Rawson for her enthusiasm and assistance, to Howard Kalish for additional illustrations, and special thanks to Ben and Marcia Schonzeit for continuous aid and support, both moral and material.

Thanks also to the following for allowing their quilts to appear: Agnes Kinard, Marilyn Frank, Judy and Glenn Greenberg, Dottie and Guy Hayes, Tom and Joy Richardson, Wendy and Alfred Sanford, and Sam Schonzeit.

CONTENTS

dow templates for hand-sewing—Diamond and hexagon templates—Appliqué templates—Blocks combining piecework and appliqué—Curved-seam templates—Constructing ⅓″ (*Illustrations by J. Gutcheon*)

The Perfect Patchwork Primer

1 THE ONCE AND FUTURE PATCHWORK QUILT

In the past few decades in this country, we have experienced an astonishing growth of interest in folk arts and handcrafts, and none has attracted more sustained, intense, or enthusiastic attention than the American patchwork quilt. Far from being a mere set of techniques with a finite number of variations and possibilities, contemporary quiltmakers have found quiltmaking to be a living tradition with an arresting past and a compelling future. American patchwork quilting is a craft with a soul, engaging not only our eyes and hands but also our imagination and our sense of history.

Quiltmaking was a standard and necessary function of every American household from the earliest days of the Massachusetts Bay Colony to the last half of the 19th century. It began to decline as improved heating made many layers of bedding less essential than they had been and machine-made blankets and comforters became available. By the twenties, machine technology was king. Scott and Zelda danced on the roofs of taxicabs, money talked and oh you kid; making things by hand became a sign of poverty, something to be ashamed of. People who still knew how to quilt denied it, put away their quilting frames and bought comforters from Sears Roebuck, like all their friends—God forbid they should be different from their friends.

Fifty years of Future Shock have dramatically reversed that modish contempt for the work of human hands. Along with a number of other neglected crafts, the art of patchwork quilting has revived with a vengeance, and the very technology boom which caused its eclipse is at least in part responsible. Since World War II, advances in colorfast dye processes and production of nonshrink dress goods have greatly reduced the problems that plagued the old-time quiltmaker.

Dacron batting, the first new quilt filler since the 18th century, has at last eliminated the need for quilting over every inch of the coverlet, opening up design possibilities undreamed of 30 years ago, and making it possible for almost anyone to do her/his own quilting. Cotton-covered polyester thread, with the girth of lightweight cotton and the tensile strength of button cord, simplifies machine-sewing, and modern quilting thread, which is coated with silicone to prevent knotting, eases quilting (and all hand-sewing) about 1000 percent.

Modern quiltmakers derive inspiration and information from the experience of their forebears, and yet, because dacron is not cotton, because silicone is not wax, because Nixon is not Queen Victoria and the 1970s are not the 1840s, it is inevitable that they are also adapting the old ways to their own tastes and needs. Truly, the current patchwork boom is not a revival, an exercise in romance or nostalgia; rather it is a new and vigorous phase of a perennial American tradition, using different tools, expressing different aspects of ourselves, and based upon a different store of information.

It is also inevitable that books written by and for the pre-war, pre-dacron, pre-crafts boom, pre-baby boom, pre-TV dinner, pre-women's-movement market, cannot adequately fill the needs of the modern quiltmaker. This book has been written to close this information gap, to link the history and experience of the traditional quiltmaker with the tastes, capabilities, and limitless possibilities of the quiltmaker of today.

To explain this, it must be made clear that our reasons for making quilts are fundamentally different from the reasons of 1840. We no longer actually *need* quilts for utilitarian purposes, because we have blankets and so on. As for the masterpiece quilts of the past that we admire so much, they represent not only imagination and extraordinary skill, they also represent years—as many as 40 years of the maker's life. Obviously, a person who undertook such a project was aiming at more than a nifty bedspread. Such a person used a needle as often, as easily, as casually as we use a telephone; it was her duty, her comfort, her companion, her mode of self-expression. And when she undertook a project of that magnitude she was not just passing time or doing a bit of show-off needlework, she was making a statement about herself: about her skill, her patience, her ability to endure endless days of hard work and tedium for the sake of the pattern of the whole, and ultimately of her sense of her own value as a human being.

Today we have other ways of making our statements to the world. We have typewriters, telephones, more jobs, more education, fewer children, less physical hardship—perhaps better, perhaps not, but different. Therefore the modern quiltmaker tends to be more interested in an unusual design or imaginative use of color or perspective, than in the sheer number of hours required to complete a project.

By the same token, many, if not most, people in this day and age prefer to sew by machine, not to mention the fact that very few of us sew as well by hand as the average 8-year-old of 1840. Granted, traditional quilts were pieced by hand, but that was because nobody had a choice, and considering the spirit of economy that has inspired American patchwork from its earliest days, I believe the use of the sewing machine to save time and trouble is an absolutely faithful development of the tradition, not a violation of it.

Neither are we going to have any elitist hokum about its taking 70 years to learn to quilt well, or how you have to have 12 stitches to the inch, absolutely even on both sides of the quilt. Take 14 if you can and if you can't, take eight. You may not win first prize at the county fair, but you'll have a perfectly handsome, workmanlike job, and within limits, the only essential criterion should be what will satisfy *you*.

Much of the pleasure and the sense of modern quilting comes from understanding what has gone before. With that in mind I have collected the richest possible assortment of traditional patchwork blocks suitable for machine (or hand) sewing. But I think we can safely dispense with the notion that the quiltmaker's brains are in her needle. Therefore I have emphasized methods for designing your own quilts, using traditional elements or your own, rather than offering specific projects to copy. From my experience as a quiltmaker and teacher, I'll tell you which steps of the traditional process you can eliminate without sacrificing quality, and maybe I'll bully you about some details if I think it will save you trouble in the end. I'll try to help you decide what's too simple to keep you interested and what's just plain too difficult. (Only you know what's too much time or trouble for you—if you want to do a masterpiece, I'll give you plenty of suggestions. But I won't blandly offer you a pattern that is going to land you in a mental ward, without warning you first.)

Finally, as long as we're confessing that times have changed, I'm not going to give you a dozen patterns shaped like swastikas and tell you they're ancient good luck symbols or the tribal sign of the Osages. (They are, but I just don't believe you're going to make a lot of baby quilts covered with swastikas.) I promise not to emit any girlish shrieks over the pattern called Drunkard's Path ("a very wobbly pattern!"). I won't quote any of Aunt Jane of Kentucky's speech "Ain't life jest like settin' up a quilt!" and I promise not to hum a few bars of " 'Twas from Aunt Dinah's quilting party/I was seeing Nelly home." We can enjoy tradition without getting downright hokey.

People talk a surprising amount of twaddle about the romance of patchwork, especially lately. ("My, don't you wish some fairy would set those patches talkin'—what a tale they could tell!") My foot. They could tell a tale of days and months of mindless, thankless tedium, cooking food of a depressing sameness, washing and sewing and mending clothes that were forever being worn out or outgrown, frustrating days and sleepless nights with a whining child ill or dying of some disease that could have been cured by one shot of penicillin. For every block of patchwork sewn in a cheerful, sunlit kitchen while fresh pies cooled on the window sill and happy children warbled in the front yard, many more were sewn in the last numb, tired hour before sleep, when the babies were in bed and the older children could be set to help with the sewing as the last chore of their care-full day, when the heat and the light from the fire were insufficient for other work, when hands and bodies were stiff with cold and fatigue, when all had been snowbound for weeks, when the stillness of the work and of the night and of the long, deadly boring white winter brought homesickness for places and people never to be seen again, whether they were back home in Connecticut, or in Sweden or Slovakia.

Patchwork, the art of making whole cloth from bits and pieces of scraps and clothes that had been worn and mended and cut down for the children and then cut down again, was far from being the leisure-time fancy work that much needlework, including some quiltmaking, has become. Instead, it was a craft born of the harshest necessity, a symbol of a life of hardship in which money was scarce, material goods were scarcer, and all one had to give was labor and time. Patchwork is really the blues of the American woman. The blues as a musical form was created by and for suffering—the blues is the feeling and the blues is what makes it bearable. The style is crude as the available instruments were crude, and the content is simple, as pain and rage and sorrow are simple. The men and women who first made the blues did so for crude and simple reasons; they had to make something just for themselves, to prove to themselves that they were human, and it had to be beautiful so their souls would have something to live on. The women who first made figures and patterns to relieve the random ugliness of early patchwork were responding to the same kind of need. Like the bluesmakers, they never thought of themselves as artists; they worked in a crude and simple medium, striving physically and spiritually to get through today on the off chance that tomorrow would be worth it. Patchwork became both the symptom and the cure for what life demanded of the American woman.

Unquestionably, the current popularity of quiltmaking is connected in time and spirit with feminist consciousness-raising, the new pride and respect women have learned to feel for themselves and each other in the last few years. For quilt-making is a feminine art, but feminine in the sense that its history is of a piece with all that is tough and independent and creative in the history of American women. For that reason, women who wouldn't go near a ladies' bridge luncheon feel perfectly comfortable in a women's quilting group, and women who have always enjoyed their bridge parties feel that making a quilt has more to do with who they are as women than making a needlepoint cummerbund from a kit. And by the same token, men who once felt obliged to scorn such "women's work" are now at ease with what is simply a proud American tradition, since they've noticed that just as man's history is woman's, woman's is also man's.

Men have at least as great a need for the simplicity and relaxation of handcrafts as women and children do, but some, perhaps understand-ably, feel a certain reticence about crocheting doi-lies on the subway. Quiltmaking, however, need have none of that frilly delicacy about it. The tools of the craft are pencils and rulers, compasses and protractors, scissors and sewing machines; it's really no more "ladylike" than building a chair. Quiltmaking is certainly a feminine art, in the sense that its most skillful practitioners have tradi-tionally been women. But men have always sewn and for that matter, have always made quilts. The Shelburne Museum in Vermont has a spectacular counterpane made by a convalescent Civil War veteran which many people, myself among them, consider to be the gem of the collection.

1. Civil War Counterpane 96″ × 111″. Built around a square central medallion with alternating borders of piecework and appliqué. Courtesy of the Shelburne Museum, Inc., Shelburne, Vt.

16

Of course the popularity of quiltmaking has also to do with our society's general appetite for handcrafts of all kinds. As the pressure and competition of overpopulation make it increasingly difficult for the individual to identify and distinguish her-himself, the industrial age has also introduced a kind of abstraction into our lives, complicating our sense of the value of time, of things, and of ourselves. We know how much an hour we get paid for our time, but does it have to do with how much we need, or how much we deserve, or how much we can get? I can spend what I make on a bedspread at Bloomingdale's, but does the price have to do with the beauty of it, or its durability, or with the hours it took to make it, or what *they* can get for it, or with the tariff on Japanese textiles?

There is a strong backlash developing against this abstract quality of modern life, this confusion about the real value of our skills and our work and our time. Some feel the release lies in returning to the land, whether for weekends, for summers, or for life. Some climb mountains or sail backwards around the world, and thousands more are slightly soothed by reading about them.

People are seeking activities that offer a direct, simple relationship between what they put in and what they get out, and are hunting for projects with a definite beginning and a definite ending, since so much of modern life seems merely a holding action—a set of routines which never began and never will end and at bottom don't seem to matter to anybody. In a world screaming from incurable pains and insoluble problems people are seeking problems they *can* solve, problems which will truly challenge but not defeat them. On every hand one sees evidence of an enormous need to master something, be it the untamed wilderness or the art of sensuous massage.

And for many of us, when we want something pure and simple in our lives, the answer is to make things with our hands. People who work in their homes are escaping their endless love-hate relationship with their labor-saving devices—those devices which have not only taken the drudgery out of housework but also taken the skill and honor out of doing it well, and they are taking up candlemaking, batik, tie-dye, Szechuan cooking, and pottery. People who work their brains out in offices all day are skipping dinner to get to evening quilt classes or leather workshops or courses in fixing the Volkswagen. Working with your hands is a restorative. It offers a release from tension, whether from overwork or boredom, a way of passing time or keeping it, a one-to-one relationship between time and achievement. Working with your hands gives you a chance not only to create or restore an object, but also to restore and re-create yourself, for when you've finished you are not just the person who endlessly makes the coffee or treks to the laundromat or pays the rent or buys the baby's shoes—you are also the person who made the thing. You have added something new, something possibly beautiful, to the world and to your life. You are what you do.

Of all the skills and crafts that have been invented or rediscovered in the last few years, there are a number of special reasons that quiltmaking has an especially great appeal. Perhaps most important, there is no other craft that I know of which is so accessible to people with no particular artistic training or ability. It's all very well to be able to knit and purl without dropping stitches, but many people really long for something more. They want to invent something of their own and they actually don't want it to look as if it were designed for the Hunchback of Notre Dame. (John and Yoko Lennon are fond of telling people that everyone is an artist, there's no such thing as a person who can't be an artist. It's very sweet and generous of them to keep saying so, and of course they're right, we are all artists, it's just that so few of us are *good* artists.)

Quiltmaking, and particularly patchwork,

offers satisfaction and scope to almost anyone. The design can be as simple or as complex, as traditional or as original as you want it; the simplest designs can be as effective as the intricate, and the most elaborate designs can nevertheless be the easiest to sew. And no matter how simple or traditional a pattern, the effect of the quilt is still absolutely original because no two people handle fabric and color the same way. And when you're done, even if the museums aren't beating down your door for it, a quilt will *work*. It will be warm and soft and one sleeve will not be eight inches longer than the other and it will not taste like broiled sneakers. And you'll know how to make the next one better.

I find that quiltmaking also has other advantages. Like a lot of people, I've been experimenting with crafts and hand-skills for a long time. Some, like knitting and macramé, were both too easy and too hard—too easy to master the basic knots and stitches, too hard to do anything really original with them. Cooking is fun but it so often leads to eating. I made a lot of shirts for my husband and even two suits, one of which he actually wears, but in the end, no matter how artfully I learned to roll the lapels, I felt I was really only following someone else's directions. Quiltmaking seemed to me the best of all possible worlds, because it is always original, it is not monotonous, it involves lots of different processes and endless variations and the actual sewing is rarely picky or difficult. It also leaves you a choice of working by hand or machine and it can be as blissfully solitary or as social as you want it. People can work together on a single quilt, or together on separate quilts, or in corners by themselves—as you like it. It's a lovely, soothing pastime for anyone who is sick in bed, as well as a perfect project for families, since families more than any other kind of group have special needs for both privacy and togetherness.

Too much cannot be said, I think, about the importance of sharing work. We've all heard a lot lately about the beleaguered condition of modern marriage and the nuclear family, and it seems to me that the quality of friendship in modern society is in a good deal of hot water as well. So many conditions are brought to bear upon it: whether your friends are married or single, who has more money, who is too smart for whom, whether you like each other's children, politics, profession, nutritional habits, racial and sexual prejudices. We try to bind ourselves to one another with shared amusement; we play bridge or golf or tennis together, we laugh together and eat and drink together, even sleep together, and behind it all there seems to be a desperation, a sense that if one condition changes, all the good times in the world won't keep the friendship from drifting away like smoke. People seem to be silently asking each other, "But what if I really *needed* you? What if I suddenly were married (or single)? What if I were broke? What if I got a disgusting disease? What if I get old?"

Surely one of the things we have lost, with the passing of the extended family and the vanished solidarity of small town life, is the habit of sharing work. We've lost a lot of other things which no one could regret, like Mad Aunt Hedy living for years in the best guest room, and all the neighbors kibitzing about the way we tie our shoes. But we've also lost the concept that a good way to express caring was to do a job of work together. Time spent in friendship was time spent building a barn, or getting in the harvest, or quilting a quilt; it seemed to foster a more stable sense of community than many people feel today, and for good reason. After all, you must have a great deal of faith in someone's affection for you to have the nerve to ask him to help you build a barn. It's a much heavier commitment than asking him to dinner, and it must go without saying that you would do the same for him. For those who have rediscovered the pleasure of sharing and exchanging labor, quilting is a natural occupation, for it gives plenty of scope for good talk as well as good work.

In an effort to discover why the trend back to patchwork is occurring precisely *now*, for several months I asked all my students why they wanted to make quilts. Some said that they had always wanted to make a quilt, often to replace one remembered from childhood, but they never had a way to learn. Some said they were good with their hands and liked to collect new crafts, and some said they couldn't sew a button on but suspected (rightly) that patchwork was something they could master. A lot of those asked, including most of the men, just felt strongly about giving hand-made gifts and believed that quilts would be nice to make and give. Some people specifically wanted something to teach to and share with their parents or children; a fair number bring their parents or children to take the class with them. One woman wanted to teach quiltmaking to her church guild so they could make quilts together and then sell them for charity. Some people came with their friends; some wanted a place of their own to go to *without* all their friends and family, to be by themselves and learn something new. And some frankly had no idea; they had seen the famous 1971 quilt show at the Whitney Museum in New York, or an article in the paper, or just felt it in the air.

I can't help suspecting at least one more reason that this particular American craft has surfaced again at this peculiar point in American history. Our country, we all know, is suffering a crisis of the spirit. We have just completed a decade in which we waded deeper and deeper into an ignoble and humiliating war, in which we shot most of our heroes and some of our children, and we've regretted it, we've been saddened by it, we've apologized till we're tired. Now more than at any time in our history we want to connect with what is still admirable and untarnished in our history. In these times there seems to be some logic in participating in a tradition that is simple and noble and American in the way we used to understand the word.

Many Americans have responded to the

disappointments of the last decade with a renewed fascination for the arts, crafts and domestic techniques of America's infancy. Prices for objects of American folk art have skyrocketed, and stores are filled with books and kits to enable you to dip your own candles as the colonials did or to dye your own homespun with onion skins and butternuts.

The revival of interest in the patchwork quilt is clearly related to this impulse, but in the case of the quiltmakers there is more at work than simple revival. The evolution of the patchwork quilt has always been closely involved with the whole social development of America, and it continues to be so. As it might be said that our public consciousness is beginning to come of age, so is the tradition of American quiltmaking.

Quiltmakers have grown past their fascination with the technical problem of How To Do It, to an interest in Why To Do It. The modern quiltmaker can easily use modern fabrics, products, and machines to insure excellent and enduring workmanship; for him or her, the challenge and satisfaction lies in the realm of esthetics and self-expression. We shall not return to the particular styles and achievements of our forebears; to want to would be silly romanticism. Instead we accept and respect what we have learned from them about How To Do It, as well as what their quilts can teach us about beauty and perseverance. Then we use these lessons to push the tradition a step forward, to say something new about ourselves, and about quiltmaking.

America, after all, is still a young country (though beginning to be old in the experience of power). She has only a few really indigenous art forms: perhaps only jazz, the blues, and the patchwork quilt. Of these, the patchwork quilt is the oldest and has suffered the longest decline, which makes it the prodigal, enjoying an explosive homecoming. Modern quiltmakers are bringing to their craft a new maturity, reflecting their spirits and their times, and there is even reason to expect that some of the best of the tradition is yet to come.

2 HISTORY

Traditional American patchwork quilts involved not one craft, but two or three. What we usually call patchwork, making a large sheet of fabric by sewing smaller pieces to each other, is called piecework in quilting parlance. This is to distinguish it from appliqué, the process of sewing small pieces onto a larger piece, which is called patchwork because it resembles the technique for mending a fabric by sewing a patch over the tear. The third process is quilting—the technique of joining two or more layers of fabric with lines of stitches.

Patching is surely as old as clothing, but the other two, piecing and quilting, are actually concepts with histories. Both were known to the ancient Egyptians. There are descriptions of bed canopies, sails, and other things pieced together from different-colored cloth and animal hides dating from as early as 10,000 B.C. The Chinese, and the Egyptians, were quilting fabric for winter clothing probably even before that.

During the Crusades, European soldiers learned from the North Africans that quilted clothing could serve as a kind of rudimentary armor, as well as protective underclothing for chain mail, if they were lucky enough to have chain mail. At home, the idea was quickly turned to domestic uses. Winter garments and bedclothes were quilted, of course, and quilting for formal attire eventually because *de rigueur* during the Spanish Bombast period (1545–1620), when it was the fashion to ornament clothing so heavily with jewels that a single layer of fabric couldn't support them.

Few examples of the craft have survived from this period, but the fact of its existence can be found in some of the best-known legends of the time. Mary Stuart, Queen of Scots, is known to have spent some of her time in imprisonment quilting coverlets. Her cousin, Queen Elizabeth, while possibly not a quilter, favored clothes of the

Spanish Bombast variety; her skirts were so heavy with ornaments that they had to be mounted on little wheels to allow her to walk.

Almost everyone knows that all Shakespeare left his wife was the second-best bed and furnishings. Most people find his will significant not because of the bed or the wife but because it is one of the few proofs we have that Wm. Shakespeare could, in fact, write. But never mind, the bed is also worth mentioning, because the second-best bed was really the comfortable one (the first-best being a formal thing for guests only) and the "furnishings" were almost surely a whole set of matching quilts, quilted canopies, and side curtains. It was bully of him to leave them to her since she probably made them herself.

It seems likely that piecework of some kind was also being done in Europe at this time. Some say piecework went from England and Holland to the New World; some say the opposite way round, not that it matters. The early history of the American patchwork quilt follows quite logically and organically the history of the earliest Americans themselves.

For a number of reasons, Europe had gotten the impression that America was always like Virginia in summer. The colonists arrived believing they had found a natural and political Utopia. John Winthrop said of the colonies, "We shall be as a city upon a hill; the eyes of the whole world will be upon us." Before the first spring, more than half of them were dead of starvation and pneumonia. They were undersupplied and unprepared for almost everything in the first years, desperately in need of ways to repair or replace what they had brought with them and to invent what they had not foreseen the need of.

From the Indians the colonists learned certain ways to deal with the environment—how to build quonset-like huts, what to do with corn, how to sprout beans in the dead of winter so they'd have enough greens to prevent scurvy until spring. From the Mother Country they got the Navigation Acts, laws designed to protect England's trade monopolies, particularly in textiles. It became illegal for the colonists to buy textiles from any country but England. It was also illegal for them to manufacture any themselves. In fact, it was illegal for anyone trained in the textile trades to emigrate to America; if you so much as knew how to build a spinning wheel you could be imprisoned for attempting it, and if they caught you a second time they cut off your hand, or your head.

In these early years, life for the colonists threatened to be nasty, brutish, and short. It was during this time that the crazy quilt, most American of all patchwork, was invented. Clothes and bedclothes were used till they fell apart, cut down for the children and used again, and at last cut up to salvage every usable scrap and sewn together to serve as bedding. Quilts were stuffed with whatever came to hand—dried leaves, shreds and rags, letters or paper—and far from being the gaudy, decorative things we know from the Victorian era, they must in many ways have symbolized the hardship and frustration of the early years in New England.

Life went on, of course. Contraband tools for textile manufacturing were built or smuggled in, sheep were raised, flax cultivated. By mid-century three colonies had passed laws in defiance of the Navigation Acts requiring every woman and child to spin a certain amount of flax each day. Coverlets could be stuffed with fleece, which was surely warmer than rags or paper, although when heated or damp it gave off the aroma of sheep. Best of all, cottons began to be exported to both England and America by the East India Company, accompanied by the anguished howls of the British wool and flax interests.

By the turn of the century producing and importing cotton was made illegal in England and the colonies, which had about the same effect as our own Prohibition—bootleggers had a field day. By

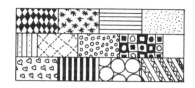

1729 it was illegal even to wear cotton, and by 1736 the laws were everywhere so flagrantly violated that they all had to be repealed. In their place a new set of taxes was imposed on the colonies so that a length of fabric cost about four times what it did in England, and an additional tax had to be paid by anyone using a spinning wheel or loom at home. Tea, you will observe, was not the only source of irritation at the Boston Tea Party.

All this economic head-squeezing obviously had a direct effect on colonial home life. While her European counterpart was raising the Italian art of trapunto quilting to new heights, the colonial woman was lucky if she could secure her quilt with a few knots through the leaves or corn cobs. But she was making a virtue of her limitations in another area, the field of patchwork design. The moment she could afford to lose an inch or two of fabric she began to cut her scraps and patches into shapes in order to bring up a pattern here and there in the grim-colored sea of motley. It may not have been much more beautiful than the crazy quilt at first, but at least it was a show of spirit. *Bricks* and *Hit or Miss* are likely examples of these early patterns. They are scrap quilts, which means they do not require any consistency of pattern or color, but rather an overall blend of many fabrics.

The second important innovation in this period was the idea of building the work not piece by piece until it formed an entire sheet, but in smaller lap-sized units which were completed separately, and then joined together to form a sheet. The original motive must have been simple convenience. Colonial women did not have the storage space, the work space, or the leisure, to sit about sewing teensy little diamonds onto the edge of something the size of three of our beds. (Colonial quilts tended to be enormous; the entire family usually slept in one room, the younger children in bed with their parents and the rest on trundles which were stored under the master bed during the day. The quilts then had to cover the large bed and

3. *Hit or Miss*

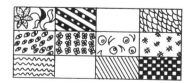

4. *Honeycomb,* an English hexagon one-patch

5. *Stained Glass,* an English hexagon pattern set with squares (technically a two-patch)

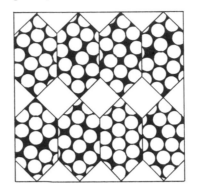

6. *Octagons,* another English two-patch

7. *Checkerboard*

8. *Roman Stripe Zig-Zag*

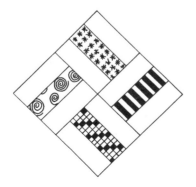

9. *Double 9-patch*

hang down far enough to conceal the trundles beneath.)

From these two ideas came the single most important innovation in American patchwork; a design contained in a single block which is repeated to make an overall pattern in the quilt top. European patchwork, then and now, was based on the one-shape design concept, called one-patch. Not that the patches were always as simple as the rectangles in *Bricks;* every conceivable shape was tried, and there were all sorts of elegant ways to set them together. But the fact remains that even when they were scrap quilts these were designed with the knowledge that you could go to the store and buy what you needed in the way of set material or extra colors and that you could work on it in a ladylike fashion in your nice clean parlor without a lot of Indians attacking you or whatever. The repetitive block design seems to be more engaging both for its causes and its effects.

The first and simplest of these designs were either four-patches, like *Checkerboard* or *Roman Stripe Zig-Zag;* or nine-patches; so called because they divide themselves into either four or nine equal squares. They too were made of scraps and were hard-used, with the result that they were worn to rags or stuffed again into other quilts and almost none have survived. We know what they looked like only because the patterns were named and loved and passed along and used again and again even to the present day. But from the middle of the 18th century we began to have masterpiece quilts that have survived and can be seen in restorations and museums.

About those intimidating museum pieces, it is useful to note that there has always been a distinction between masterpiece and utility quilts. When you see an old quilt that makes you want to turn in your thimble and watch television, remember that its survival suggests that its owners felt that it was almost too good to use. These colonial masterpiece quilts were elaborately planned, usually around a central panel or medallion, with a series of intricate border strips building outward in concentric squares. The medallion was sometimes pieced, but more often it was printed with a copperplate picture, or had a copperplate spray of flowers or fruit cut from another fabric and appliquéd onto it. The popular fabric was chintz, and the copperplate prints were those baroque kinds of things that look like wallpaper.

If the business of cutting out a picture from one piece of fabric just to attach it to another seems a bit much, keep in mind that imported chintz and domestic oiled cotton were either illegal or very expensive, and before 1750 all prints had to be handblocked. The first American fabric printer opened in Boston in 1712, the second, opening a year or so later, ran newspaper ads saying his printing was more accurate and imaginative and didn't smell nearly as bad. The discovery in 1750 that copperplate printing could be used on fabric was a major breakthrough. No one mentions how it smelled, but it was infinitely faster, more exact, and cheaper than hand printing with wooden blocks.

American appliqué quilts began in 1750 with those copperplate bouquets, and patches or not, they have always been held the aristocrats of American quilts. In later years a pioneer woman often began two quilts at once, an appliqué to be worked on only when she was well-rested and the light was good, and a pieced quilt to be worked on whenever she had a free moment. The latter was slapped together and used at once. Keep in mind that quilts were really the only bedding available; blankets were not mass-produced much before the Civil War, and machine-made comforters weren't sold until about 1890. Also a number of quilts were needed for each bed, since a colonist's idea of a toasty-warm room was about 55° in the daytime, much colder at night.

After 1750 it is fruitless to think about the development of quiltmaking chronologically, because the really dramatic movement of America

10. Bowknots and Swags, 81″ × 93″. A late 18th-century medallion coverlet. The flowers and peacocks in the white spaces are made from tiny pieces of chintz applied with cross-stitch and decorated with crewel wool embroidery. The floral motif on each swag is cut from hand-painted cotton. The border rows are pieced from chintz squares and triangles. Courtesy of the Shelburne Museum, Inc., Shelburne, Vt.

11. *Duck's Foot—Bear's Paw*

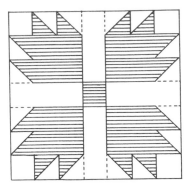

12. *LeMoyne Star*

13. *Tippecanoe*

in the 18th and 19th centuries was not through time, but through space. While elegant medallion-style quilts were made in Boston and Philadelphia, primitive crazy quilts and one-patches were made in cabins in Ohio. When refinement came to Pittsburgh and Cincinnati, frontier women pushed on to sod huts on the plains and a life every bit as deprived, isolated, and challenging as that of Massachusetts Bay.

Of course, certain historical points are essential to a collector concerned with dating or naming an antique quilt. For instance, there were no reliable green dyes before 1813, so a green fabric that has washed out leaving blue or yellow is probably 18th century. Similarly, if a cotton filler from before 1792 (the invention of the cotton gin) is relatively free of seeds, one can assume that the owner was wealthy enough to own slaves to clean the cotton. If the quilt is seed-free and dates from between 1800 and 1840, when the gin was really perfected, one might further assume that the maker lived in the South, which in turn affects the probable name of some blocks.

The correct name of the quilt depends a great deal on locale. A patch known as *Duck Foot in the Mud* on Long Island is known simultaneously as *Hand of Friendship* in Quaker Philadelphia and as *Bear's Paw* in Ohio. A block named *Jacob's Ladder* in Puritan New England appears the same or slightly varied in the West as *Road to Oklahoma* and later as *Road to California*.

There is a popular block made of diamonds called *LeMoyne Star*, named after the LeMoyne brothers who founded New Orleans. However, the LeMoynes grew more and more unpopular outside Louisiana as they claimed more and more land for France, thus, their block was usually called *Lemon Star* in the North. Some call it bad French, some suspect sour grapes.

The block called *Tippecanoe* (there are lots of blocks named for historical events) is similar to the block called the *Rocky Road to Kansas*, suggesting

perhaps that while half the people worried about Harrison beating Tyler the rest were wondering how soon the covered wagon would break another axle. But I'm sure you can dream your own dreams about quilt names and you don't need me to twitter, "And land sakes, here's one called *Indian Hatchet* shaped like the hatchet of an Indian." More important than the quilt names, I think, is the meaning of the activity of quiltmaking to the women who pursued it.

In *Old Patchwork Quilts and the Women Who Made Them*, Ruth Finley quotes a letter from a woman in Ohio writing to her sister in Connecticut the winter after that same Harrison was elected. She said that after being snowed in all winter, the roads had been cleared enough for one of her neighbors to send word asking her to a party to quilt the tops she had pieced over the winter. It snowed again the day of the party but they were able to get through, and her husband had a chance to spend the evening talking with his friends about the new Whig president. The hostess had made two quilt tops, one in a pattern no one had seen before, and there was a turkey for dinner. The writer remarked that it made her remember oysters and cranberries; they never got oysters or cranberries in Ohio, nor would they. She had brought six squash pies; all her pumpkins had froze.

For women in rural communities and frontier areas the "quilting party" was a ritual of great importance. Life was too harsh to allow much socializing for mere companionship, and people left the demands of their own jobs at home only for church or when there was a communal job of work to be done. Such jobs were usually house or barn raisings, harvest or corn husking, occasions when you arrived at dawn in your oldest clothes, cooked all day for sixty instead of for eight, and in general worked even harder than usual. Only the quilting bee gave a woman a chance to dress up a little, to spend a day in company with her friends and to work at something to be used more gratefully and remembered longer than last summer's pickled beets. It was an occasion for a great deal of talk and even of competition, for only six or at most eight people could work at a frame at once, and whoever was found to be least adept ran the risk of having to stuff the turkey. There was "dinner" at noon for the ladies, and a supper at night for everyone, followed by games and dancing and a lot of significant snuggling behind the forsythia bush, if one is to believe the songs and stories.

It is easy to imagine why the quilting bee was a potent emotional occasion. For a woman who had been isolated all winter, with only men and children for company, there was the chance to meet her friends again. The luxury of working purely for her own satisfaction must have been a great luxury indeed. For younger women, the occasion was very often an engagement party. Children were taught to sew very early, about the age ours are learning to change channels for themselves, and by the time she was old enough to marry, a girl was expected to have finished a dozen quilt tops for her hope chest. When she became engaged, she invited her friends and family to a party to quilt the tops and to plan a special bride quilt, which they would all make together. The bride quilt was generally appliquéd with hearts and lover's knots and all sorts of things that were bad luck for anyone not properly spoken for.

Such quilts were really speaking things to their makers and owners, and superstition and symbolism were a natural part of their language; these aspects of quilts convey a good deal about the minds and lives of their makers. There's a difference, for example, between feeling sentimental about weddings and being downright superstitious. Marriage was not something a girl dreamed about along with a vision of herself nursing the sick or running for Congress; it was virtually her only option. Not to marry may be thought a misfortune now, but in those days it was a disaster. A girl planned for it, she prayed for it, and she certainly

didn't sew any hearts or lover's knots on anything until she was entitled to.

There is a handsome patch called *Wandering Foot* which was considered so dangerous a carrier of wanderlust that it was never used on a quilt for a young person. We are apt to forget that in a time of low literacy, infrequent and expensive mail service, and no other communication but word of mouth, a child who decided to wander was virtually lost to his/her family. In fact, the phrase "So-and-so's gone West" came to mean that so-and-so had died. Eventually *Wandering Foot* was renamed *Turkey Tracks* in an effort to foil the jinx.

The Pennsylvania Dutch, whose famous hex signs are still seen on barns throughout their area, as a group were the most proficient and original American quiltmakers. Their designs tend to be bold and brightly colored, like their hex signs, and they especially favored patterns with curved seams (which are by far the most difficult to piece). Incidentally, Pennsylvania Dutch women were not taught to read and write; needlework was their only means of leaving a lasting record of themselves.

In some areas there was a superstitious belief that to make a perfect quilt was offensive to God, that He would feel the quiltmaker was setting up in competition with Him. Consequently you often see beautifully intricate old quilts with something idiotically wrong with them, like a tree upside down. It makes you think a bit about that particular relationship with God, and it also comes in handy when you've got your whole king-size quilt all quilted and suddenly notice the third block in the second row is in backward.

During the 19th century, as life styles changed and conditions eased, symbolism in quilts became more and more sophisticated. Quiltmaking became more of a leisure activity and less a necessity of life. More ceremonial quilts were made as wedding gifts, going-away presents, tokens of esteem to outgoing ministers and incoming presidents, as well as lugubrious affairs called Memory Quilts made from the clothes of the departed, and fancy Best Quilts for honored guests only (like the Elizabethan first-best bed). More and more these quilts were appliquéd and quilted with symbols that spoke volumes to the users, for the 19th century was the age of symbols, as ours is the age of mass media. Whole monographs have been written on the implications of the pineapple. (Used especially for guest quilts, it was a sign of hospitality.)

What the appliqué quilt gained in status the useful pieced quilt lost. In the latter half of the century there developed a rage for all-white quilts, focusing attention entirely on the quilting, which was always elaborate, sometimes padded in the Italian style. Those who couldn't make or buy an all-white quilt turned over their humble pieced quilts to display the white underside, and pretended.

At the same time another rage swept England and America like the hula hoop: the vogue of the Victorian Crazy Quilt. The Victorian Crazy Quilt was the brontosaurus of American patchwork. It was a logical extension of all that had gone before, and while it was an evolutionary dead end, it achieved some rather spectacular specimens before it expired in mothballs. Fig. 16 shows one made by my great-grandmother, called the *Grand Army Quilt*, featuring eagles, flags, military insignia embroidered in gold, and ribbons from her father's Civil War medals. Typical of its kind, it is made of silks and velvets and has no batting since the type and variety of fabrics would make it impossible to quilt. The pieces are held in place with decorative lines of crewelwork in silk thread representing flowers, stars, sheaves of wheat, and so on, and most of the pieces are further decorated with crewel or embroidery. Notice the two flags in the central medallion, and the spider web and mallard duck to the right.

With the fragile, decorative, virtually unusable Victorian Crazy Quilt, American quiltmaking

16. *Grand Army Quilt*, 68″ × 68″. Made by Minnie Sherman, c. 1880.

had turned completely away from its source and marched firmly into a corner. Machine-made blankets and comforters made quiltmaking unnecessary; the tastes of the times made it downright frivolous. In some areas, knowing how to quilt became a sign of poverty and a source of shame; in others, people vied with one another to see how many quilting stitches they could plaster a quilt with, or how many teeny little pieces they could sew together. (The record holder, a man as it happens, made a quilt with something like 53,000 hexagons in it.) Quiltmaking had managed to place itself on a par with swallowing live goldfish.

There was something of a revival during the Depression. Parks Departments set women to quilting, just as they put their husbands to landscaping highways, but the movement was not self-propelled and not long-lived. In the late sixties there appeared a genuine rebirth of interest in quiltmaking not as a leisure-time activity but once again as respectable, responsible work. A black group in the South formed the Martin Luther King Freedom Quilting Bee to make patchwork quilts to sell in shops and department stores, and a similar group in West Virginia called Mountain Artisans makes patchwork clothes, pillows, and comforters for national distribution. Beautiful and original quilting is being done in some rural communes, and the Dakotah group, whose quilts are now available in metropolitan department stores, work in original designs based on Indian motifs. (About two-thirds of the women involved are Plains Indians.)

Among private quiltmakers, the current emphasis is on good workmanship, of course, but more particularly on innovative design, which creates a problem of classification that would have vastly amused our foremothers. Is quiltmaking a craft, a folk-art, an art, or all of them, or none? If it is an art, does that make it Art? The relationship between patchwork and graphic design is obvious, yet people feel there is some impenetrable barrier between arts and crafts and insist that they know the difference. The difference is evidently the medium, for painters execute patchwork blocks in oil and no one is confused. But does a well-designed quilt belong in a gallery or a department store? Should it be priced as a graphic design or as a bedspread?

Unfortunately, it is very difficult for some people to know how to value things if they cannot categorize them, yet it is clear that quilts can be valuable on more than one level. John Dewey, in *Art as Experience*, poses the problem of a shapely mineral lump which is placed in the art museum as the work of a primitive artist, but must be moved to the museum of natural history when it is found to have been shaped by natural forces. Why, since it is the same lump as before the discovery? Dewey's reason is that art is an esthetic experience transmitted from the artist to the beholder, and in that sense quiltmaking is most certainly an art. The difference between the natural lump and the primitive statue is like the difference between a factory bedspread and a handmade quilt. The first things are only themselves, for one does not communicate with a machine or a mass of igneous gasses. But the statue and the quilt are more than themselves; they represent also the experience of making them. Whether quiltmaking is a craft or an art, it is above all an experience shared, not only by the maker and the perceiver of any particular quilt but by all the makers of all the quilts. The experience of the modern quiltmaker is greatly enriched by the experience of all who have gone before and he/she is in turn enlarging the experience available to quiltmakers to come. That, if I understand it, is the definition of a tradition.

3   DEFINITIONS

ALBUM QUILT

A quilt in which each block is made by a different person, couple, or group, and signed with either embroidery stitching or indelible ink. Special patchwork patterns with a blank space in the middle for the signature were sometimes used. Each maker worked the same pattern in his/her choice of fabric. They were usually made as going-away presents, or as a gesture of special regard.

ALL-WHITE QUILT

Popular from mid-19th century on. A completely white spread made to exhibit fancy quilting of every conceivable kind. The pattern was often arranged around a central figure, such as a basket of fruit, and the most prestigious included padded or trapunto quilting, at least in the central portion.

APPLIQUÉ

From the French, meaning "applied." Also called applied work, laid-on work, and patchwork. To appliqué is to sew a small piece of fabric to a larger one. An appliqué is the piece to be applied.

BACKSTITCH

A stitch used in hand-sewing either to strengthen a line of stitching or to secure the thread at the beginning or end. To backstitch: (a) take a short stitch on the underside; (b) reinsert the needle at the beginning of the first stitch and bring it up a stitch length ahead.

BACKING

The bottom or lining layer of a quilt or comforter. Made first of homespun, now usually muslin.

17. Backstitch

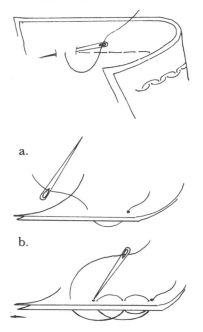

a.

b.

40

BASTE

To secure temporarily. Usually done with long running stitches, or with pins.

BATTING

Also called filler, stuffing, or wadding. The fluffy middle layer of the quilt, batting creates warmth by providing insulation. It also enhances the quilting by puffing up slightly around the line of stitches (which a woven filling does not.) Once made of woolen fleece, it is now either cotton or dacron.

BINDING

A strip of fabric hemmed to the back and front to enclose the raw edges of material; a common device for finishing blankets or quilts.

BLOCK

A unit of patchwork design, usually square, used alone or repeated to build an overall pattern in a quilt top.

CALICO

Originally, cotton imported by the East India Company of Calicut; later any cotton cloth closely printed in bright colors, usually in a flower print. It became the staple of American quiltmakers for 100 years, partly because it was available, partly because the tiny scale of the print showed to such advantage when cut in little pieces. Today it is in vogue again for many of the same reasons that patchwork is. Unfortunately, the imitation calico prints are rarely done with the subtlety of the originals, and they are often used on fabrics not suitable for patchwork. Genuine calico printed on new cloth with hundred-year-old plates is available by mail; see the list of mail order sources (p. 254).

COMFORTER

Also called a puff; a heavy bedcovering filled with dacron or down.

18. Running stitch

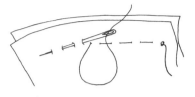

19. Pin-basting

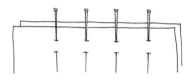

20. Binding

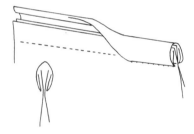

21. *Pinwheel* blocks

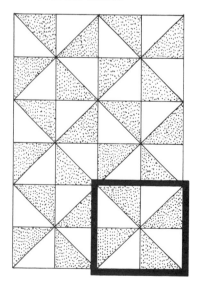

COUNTERPANE

A bedspread. From the French word for counterpoint, meaning backstitch. European quilting was usually done with backstitch, while American is almost always done in a running stitch.

COVERLET

A quilt used at night for warmth; not long enough to cover the pillows. Or in general, any bedcovering.

CRAZY QUILT

Patchwork made of random size, shape, and color pieces having no particular pattern.

EMBROIDERY

Decorative top stitches, used in patchwork to secure edges of crazy-piecing.

FREEDOM QUILT

A presentation quilt made in colonial times to honor a man on his twenty-first birthday. Achieving majority in those days was a significant event; prior to it a boy was the economic property of his parents, who could apprentice him without his consent and could take everything hc made. (A girl, of course, was always the property/responsibility of her parents unless or until she married, when she became the property of her husband.) The freedom quilt was usually quite a production and was put away until the young man became engaged, at which time it was added to his bride's hope chest.

FRIENDSHIP MEDLEY QUILT

A gift quilt in which each block is made by a different person or couple, and each has a different design. They were often made at quilt parties, and each block was signed by the maker. The photograph shows a quilt made at Kingston, N. Y. and dated Feb. 10, 1865. It includes fine piecework and

22. The *Abraham Lincoln* spread, 78″ × 83″. A medley quilt, having each block made and signed by a different guest at a quilt party. Shelburne Museum, Shelburne, Vt.

23. A *Blazing Star* quilt ("Sunburst" variation)

some extraordinary appliqué. Notice especially the portrait of President Lincoln, who was to be assassinated two months later, and the Lincoln-Douglas Debates block on the left, made by a Mr. Drake (who was apparently a Lincoln partisan).

HEM

n. The finished edge of a piece of sewing having the raw edge turned under and the resulting fold sewn in place.

v. To turn under a raw edge and secure with a hemming stitch, invisible on the right side. Sewing from right to left take a diagonal stitch through the top of the fold, pick up one thread above the hem, and so on. This is used to hem clothing which is only seen on the right side, and in some of the projects in the last chapter of this book.

The hemming stitch used in quiltmaking is the blind hem, which is completely invisible (in theory). It is used for appliqué and for binding or finishing the edges of the quilt. Sew a slip stitch inside and parallel to the top of the fold, pick up a thread or two just behind the fold (and thus out of sight), take another slip stitch in the fold, etc.

MASTERPIECE QUILT

A status symbol—a quilt made less to warm the body than to boggle the mind. They generally took a great deal of time, but the fineness and difficulty of the needlework was the criterion for a masterpiece even more than the time involved. (One often finds very simple utility quilts which nevertheless must have taken years because of the thousands and thousands of tiny scraps used. These speak more of economy than of skill.) In some areas the favorite masterpiece project was an enormous *Blazing Star* pieced from thousands of tiny diamonds; clumsy cutting or sewing of even a single piece could throw off the whole design. The Pennsylvania Dutch women made masterpiece quilts with apparently simple designs; the difficulty lay in the fact that they pieced acute

24.
a. Turned once   b. Turned twice

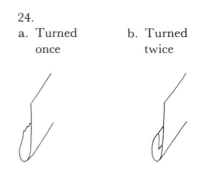

25. Hemming stitch

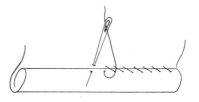

26. Blind-hemming stitch

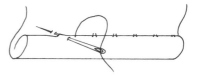

curves and arcs which any other women would have appliquéd.

In other areas, appliqué work carried the most prestige, and masterpiece quilts were elaborately planned with motifs of fruits and flowers and rows and rows of border; they were then spectacularly quilted as well. Sometimes, especially during the Victorian vogue of the all-white quilt, the masterpiece was executed in spectacular quilting alone.

A masterpiece quilt, like grandmother's Wedgwood and the heirloom silver, was generally kept in the family, and generally in mothballs except for special occasions. The honorary function of it was so well understood that to offer an unwelcome guest a pieced quilt instead of the best appliqué was a hint only slightly more subtle than locking the door behind him when he left to take a walk.

It is interesting to consider how our attitude toward masterpiece quilts has changed. The quilt show at the Whitney Museum in New York included some pieces which were very badly sewn, particularly a difficult curved-seam pattern called *Around the World* which would have been laughed out of the county fair 50 years ago; yet their masterful approach to color and design amply justified their presence in a museum of fine arts.

MEDALLION QUILT

A quilt top organized around a central motif or medallion, surrounded by a border or borders radiating outward in concentric squares.

These were especially popular in colonial times, when the central medallion might have been a particularly handsome bit of hand-blocked or printed chintz, or appliquéd with intricate figures cut from copperplate cotton and rearranged to suit the maker's fancy. They remained popular as masterpiece quilts in areas where elegantly printed cottons were available, well into the 19th century.

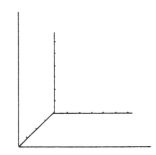

MEMORY QUILT

A mournful item made from pieces of clothing of a departed loved one. Popular in the post-Prince-Albert Victorian years, when grief was not grief if one did not visibly wallow in it.

MITER

A right angle, formed with a diagonal seam from the inside to the outside corner. It is sewn by hand, and is most often used in making borders.

PADDED WORK

Areas of quilting thrown into relief through the addition of extra padding through little holes worked in the backing. This was extremely difficult to do well, because if too little stuffing was added the effect was lost, and if too much was used, the padding might swell during washing and burst the stitches.

PATCH, n.

A term to be avoided since it means everything, therefore nothing. Used in old-time quilt parlance to mean a piece (in piecework); an appliqué (the thing to be applied); or the whole block (one speaks of the *Road to Oklahoma* patch). A one-patch is a design based on a piece of only one shape and size.

PATCHWORK

The generic term for making a large piece of cloth from smaller ones, whether by seaming pieces together as in a mosaic (piecework) or by sewing one onto another (appliqué).

Its limited meaning in quilt lingo is the second, appliqué work, for it is taken to describe sewing a patch to a whole piece as one patches a torn garment.

PIECE, v.

To sew two or more pieces of fabric together to make a larger piece.

PIECEWORK

Piecework specifically is the kind of patchwork made by seaming small pieces together to form a larger piece.

QUILT

n. A bedcovering having three layers, a decorative top sheet, a middle layer of fluffy filling about ¼″ thick, and a backing or lining layer. Properly these layers should be secured with lines of running stitches called quilting, but in fact people call almost any three-layer bed covering a quilt.

v. The act of anchoring layers of material together with multiple lines of running or back stitches.

QUILT TOP

The uppermost sheet of a quilt, either patchwork or decorated with crewel or embroidery, or plain to show off quilting.

REVERSE APPLIQUÉ

A decorative technique used particularly well and often by Central and South American Indians. The design is cut out of (rather than sewn onto) the top piece. Tiny hems are clipped and turned underneath along the inside of the pattern holes, and the piece is then applied to a background piece of a contrasting color. Often the background fabric is pieced so that different colors appear in different holes.

SET

The way in which patchwork blocks are joined to form the quilt top; i.e., piece blocks may be set with alternate plain squares or with lattice strips between them, etc.

TEMPLATE, n., a pattern

In patchwork a template is made of thin, stiff material, such as posterboard, which can be cut out with a scissor, but which will not lose its shape while being traced around repeatedly.

THROW
A small quilt or coverlet to be used as a lap rug or during a nap.

TOP-STITCH
Functional and/or decorative stitching done on the right side of the work; it is meant to show.

TRAPUNTO QUILTING
Raised or corded quilting in which the design is thrown into relief by drawing a cord into the middle layer of the work between two parallel lines of stitching.

UTILITY QUILT
A functional bedcovering; in fact, the principle bedcovering in common use in Europe and America, from the decline in popularity of animal skins in the Middle Ages to the advent of machine-made blankets in mid-19th century.

4 BEFORE YOU BEGIN

In teaching my classes in beginning quilt-making, I've found that certain basic questions about quilts, about general sewing and related matters, tend to crop up again and again. Therefore, at the risk of boring some of you, here are some things that should be understood before you begin.

HOW A QUILT IS MADE

1. A quilt is a bedcover with three layers, a top, a filling, and a backing, held together by quilting stitches. The top is usually either patchwork or appliqué or a combination of the two. The top is made first.

2. A patchwork top is usually made up of patchwork *blocks, set* together in certain ways. In the design chapter you will find over 150 examples of patchwork blocks, along with the many different ways there are to set them. The first step in making a quilt top is to draw a design on paper. You choose a patchwork block, then with colored pencils you draw it several times set together in different ways and colored in different ways, until you achieve an overall pattern you like.

3. The next step is to cut out fabric pieces to correspond with the pieces in your drawing. You do this my making *templates* (Webster defines a template as "a pattern or mold") out of cardboard the size and shape of the fabric pieces you need. You trace around these templates on the fabric until you have outlined all the pieces you need, then you cut the pieces out. Each piece must be traced and cut individually.

4. By hand or machine, sew the pieces together as shown in your drawing, first into blocks, then into rows, then into a sheet.

5. Next, you choose a pattern of quilting stitches to complement the patchwork design, and mark the quilting pattern in chalk or pencil onto the quilt top.

6. Last, you cut or piece (sew pieces together) to make a sheet of lining fabric the same size as the patchwork top. Then assemble the three layers of the quilt, lining–filling–top, and secure the three layers with lines of quilting stitches in a design of your choice. Then finish the edges.

CHOOSING FABRICS FOR PATCHWORK

Your first experiment in patchwork should be something small, like a baby's quilt or a wall hanging. This is not because there is so much practice required to perfect your construction techniques—actually, you will probably master most of the sewing on your first try, and go on botching the other things until you're 80. The one thing you can only learn by practice is a sense of how a great many fabrics go together when cut into little pieces and juxtaposed. Most people assume that combining fabrics is the one thing that will be easy, because, after all, they've been dressing themselves for years and know perfectly well what color shirt to wear with mauve plaid slacks. However, it has probably been quite a while since you wore six floral prints at the same time.

If you make your own clothes, you are used to choosing fabrics, consciously or not, that go well with your complexion and are flattering to you. When you first choose fabrics for patchwork you will automatically do the same thing. I made quite a few quilts before I realized this; when my husband was planning his first quilt he went through my precious scrap collection and said, "Where's the yellow?" There wasn't any, not because I don't like it, but because I never wear it. He went out and bought an armload of remnants in various shades of yellow and bright red, which I also don't wear, and now we're much happier.

You'll also pick up other things as you experiment. Some colors and types of prints seem to pop out at you, while others seem to recede. Some fabrics are in different *hues*—one is red while the other is green—but have the same *value*—the same intensity, the same degree of darkness or lightness. When two fabrics have the same color value they look like the same color in black and white. You can test this by placing the two side by side and looking at them with your eyes squinting almost closed. (The less light you allow in, the more your vision becomes like black and white film.) Manipulating the color values is one of the important ways to get graphic effects with patchwork and it is also something you have to learn for yourself.

Another thing you will learn only with practice is how to combine scales of print. You may have three fabrics in different colors printed with pansies, amoebas, and fire engines respectively. If each figure in the print is roughly the same size, even though the pictures are of very different things, the combination will lack one kind of texture. You would be better off with three flower figures each in a slightly different size. (If you can vary both the figure *and* the scale, so much the better.)

You will also discover that fabrics look very different cut into little pieces than they do on the bolt. Very small prints tend to work like pointillist painting technique (or the kind of printing they use for comic books): tiny points of color seen from a distance appear solid. This is a great advantage in patchwork; it enables you to create a rich texture by using a large number of dissimilar prints without clashing, but in order to make it work the way you intend it to, you must remember to stand back from the fabric and squint at it as well as examining it up close.

With large prints, you have to see a certain amount of the fabric for the print to make any sense; cut small, it might be very arty or it might just be incomprehensible. The only way to judge beforehand what the effect will be is to practice; neither does it really help to make a single sample block. You ought to see at least four blocks together to get the real hang of it. So begin with a project larger than a pillow, but not something so large and important to you that you will be disappointed if your first work isn't your best.

HAND- OR MACHINE-SEWING

There are some patterns that can only be sewn by hand. There are some patterns so complex they would take forever if not sewn by machine. There are some people who prefer one method of working to the other. Obviously, it will help you to know which patterns are which before you begin to design.

For hand-sewing buffs, traditional appliqué is always done by hand with either an invisible hemming stitch or a fine blanket stitch. If you sew well and prefer to sew by hand, it makes sense to choose or design an appliqué block or one that combines appliqué and patchwork. This will give you the greatest variety of work to do and the best chance to improve and show off your skill. But you can do any of the patterns in this book—anything that can be machine-sewn can be sewn by hand.

However, not everything that can be done by hand can be done by machine—at least not quickly or consistently well. Part of the art of modern patchwork is learning to choose or modify blocks that can be machine-sewn with speed and perfect accuracy; there is no special seat in heaven for those who choose difficult sewing jobs when a straightforward plan would have yielded an equally beautiful design.

The easiest kind of sewing is a straight-line seam. If you have done some sewing before, you know from facing necklines and setting in sleeves that it is hard to keep a curve perfectly smooth and even; this is true whether you work by hand or machine, and it is doubly true in patchwork because the curves in patchwork are likely to be much more acute than those you encounter in dressmaking. The more acute the curve, the more difficulty there will be. In general, curve-seam patchwork is graduate work, and should only be undertaken by a proficient needleperson.

28. *Day Lily* block

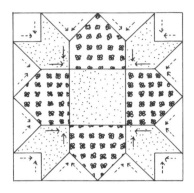

29. *Weathervane:* traditional piecing, with arrows showing where corners are set into angles

30. *Susannah*: traditional piecing

31. *Susannah*: revised for straight-seam piecing

The biggest difficulty, because it comes up most often, is the problem of setting a corner piece into an angle. To do this you have to make the seam turn a sharp corner at *exactly* the right spot. If the stitch is slightly short, there will be a gap in the patchwork when you turn it to the right side and press; if the stitch is even a little long, there will be a very obvious pucker. You can see that this would be fairly easy to control if you were sewing by hand, for you can just make the corner stitch a little longer or shorter as the case demands. But when you are sewing by machine, the needle chugs along making every stitch the same length; invariably, when you reach the corner you have to stop and adjust the work, fussing it this way and that to get it perfect. This weakens the line of stitching, takes time, and in the end you often don't get it right anyway, unless you have done a great deal of extra measuring and marking before you started to sew.

If you would just as soon avoid this problem, you have to think carefully about the way a block will be constructed when you first consider using it in your design. Imagine the block completely in pieces, then, step by step, work out how to sew it together, to see if it can be done with straight seams.

You will find that some traditional patterns, designed before machine-sewing was a possibility, could not be done with straight seams. For those, it

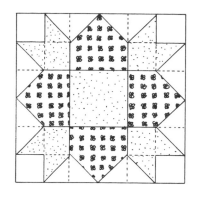

32. *Weathervane:* revised

is necessary to add seams, as I have shown with *Susannah* and *Weathervane*. This will mean more pieces to cut out and sew, balanced against all the time and annoyance that would otherwise be required to set in angle pieces. I think it is almost always worth it to adapt a pattern for machine-sewing, but some people prefer to sew the straight-seam part of the blocks by machine and set in the angle pieces by hand—a perfectly good solution if you have the patience.

Except for the curve-seam and appliqué blocks, and the few clearly labeled for hand-sewing, every block in this book is suitable for machine-sewing. In the cases where it might not be clear how to piece them using only straight lines, I have added dotted lines to indicate construction units or places where seams must be added.

THE SIZE OF THE PROJECT

The size of the project—that is, the amount of work involved—is determined by how many patchwork pieces are necessary to make up the whole quilt top, not by the size of the quilt. Some blocks have 50 or 60 pieces in them; some, equally effective, have 4 or 8. When you are choosing a block for a design, keep in mind roughly how many blocks you will need for the finished top so you can multiply it by the number of pieces in the block. Thus if you are planning a spread for a single bed with about 35 blocks, and you choose a block having 15 pieces, there will be 525 pieces in the whole top for you to trace, cut out, and sew together. If you are making a baby quilt needing only 12 blocks, but each block has 50 pieces, the baby quilt will have 700 pieces and will take you that much longer than the big one.

When I planned my first quilt, I decided to make it in a simple scrap pattern; I thought I would whip something together out of old clothes, like those stupid perky blouses I bought to take to college and never wore. Boy was I surprised! In the first place, my simple checkerboard pattern required over 1000 little square pieces —1003, to be precise, and that isn't counting the set material. My next mistake was to try to fold the material to cut out four or more squares at once. All the squares came out different-sized trapezoids, it took me two weeks, and by the time I was finished the heel of my hand was so swollen from the scissors that it was another week before I could begin to sew. The quilt turned out very nicely, as it happens, but it was eight months before I had the stomach to try another. So, my rule of thumb about size is that 300–500 pieces is a comfortable project, 700–1000 is a major opus suitable for wedding gifts and other state occasions, and over 1000 is sheer punishment. Your tolerances will probably be different from mine, but whatever they are, keep in mind and adjust the size and number and set of the blocks to stay within them. (In other words, if you have too many pieces, plan to make the block 16″ instead of 12″ so you can use fewer blocks, or make the quilt bigger by using fewer blocks with wide strips of fabric between, or make a patchwork area smaller and fill out the size with wide plain borders.)

SCRAP QUILTS

Finally, you will probably learn most if your first project is not a scrap quilt. Planning a scrap quilt is quite a different design proposition than one for which you choose a small number of fabrics to be used in a consistent way throughout the patchwork. It is true that when a colonial child made her first quilt it was usually of scraps, but that was because it was too expensive to allow her to experiment on whole cloth, not because scrap quilts are easier to handle. In fact, they can be harder to do well, because you have to make an esthetic decision each time you add a new piece and you can't see the effect, often, until it's too late. (If you get too many lights or darks clustered in one part of the quilt, it makes the top blotchy and unbalanced.) If you are deliberately manipulating dark and light for a particular effect, you cannot always tell whether a lilac calico with dark red flowers is going to read as light or dark until you have the whole thing together.

Some of the most complex and impressive of American masterpiece quilts are scrap quilts—most notably, the enormous *Blazing Star* quilts and the *Log Cabin* or *Barn Raising* patterns, which are always well represented in museum collections. For a scrap quilt that aspires to anything less than knocking your eye out, it is best to choose a simple, uncluttered block like a *Checkerboard* or *Pinwheel.* There are also a large number of blocks invented and traditionally used for scrap quilts that can be identified by name; they are called *Beggar's Block, Friendship Dahlia,* and so on, to signify that you made them by begging scraps from friends when your own collection was exhausted. (If you are using scraps, the more you can get, the better.)

5   DESIGN

TRADITIONAL CLASSIFICATIONS

In the old days, patchwork blocks were made by folding paper. They would start with a square of paper and fold it into four equal squares, making a basic four-patch, or perhaps into nine equal squares like a tic-tac-toe board, which made a nine-patch. Then they folded and cut the patches into different designs, and they had to start over with a new piece of paper if they wanted to try something different.

Anyone who has eyed an old quilt at a fair or read a quilt story in a magazine has heard a lot of knowing talk about four-patches and nine-patches, but I've found in my classes that classifying patches is very confusing to some people, at first; sorting out the basic elements of patchwork is an acquired skill, like learning to read a blueprint. Once you get used to looking at patterns and taking them apart in your mind to see how they are sewn together, the matter of how to classify them becomes perfectly clear. But in any case, it is an irrelevant piece of information to a modern quiltmaker—interesting, but irrelevant, because patchwork patterns are now designed in an entirely different way. I advise you to forget about it for the moment.

APPROACHING DESIGN

For many people, designing a quilt is the most important and interesting part of the work, yet it is usually the aspect that gets the least attention. There is something dreamy and romantic about the sewing and the quilting; you look at an old quilt and you can think about the hands that made the little stitches, and wonder what the room looked like where the work was done and what the maker was thinking about; it lends itself to tableaus. It's harder to think about the act of designing, so nobody does, much.

The best way to begin, I think, is to spend some time familiarizing yourself with what has been done before (a sensible way to introduce your-self to any new field of endeavor). Look at the pic-tures and drawings in this book, look at magazines running quilt stories, look in stores and museums for old quilts, all the time asking yourself, "How was this done? How was it designed? Which little piece was sewn first to which other piece and why?" You will soon learn to separate the individual block from the overall effect of the patchwork. Remember that before 1900 any pea-brained six-year-old could look at practically any quilt and tell at a glance how it was made. Remember, too, that the most mature and intelligent Stone Age man in Borneo sees nothing but flat grey blotches the first time he is shown a photograph. The eye must be trained to make sense out of two-dimensional designs. You learned to read pictures before you were one, just by seeing enough of them, and the chances are you can master patchwork too.

CHOOSING A BLOCK

When you first begin looking at quilts, you see the whole design at once and have to reason back-wards from that until you can see the single block or design unit from which it was made. To *design* a quilt you proceed the other way; you choose a block and build an overall pattern with it.

As you probably have discovered, the smallest design unit in a pattern can be a geometric patch-work block, or a free-form appliqué block, or even a single geometric shape like a diamond or a hexagon. For a first project I advise planning a small patchwork pattern based on a simple geometric block. Even if you are ultimately more interested in appliqué or one-patch, you will learn the most about the techniques and processes of quiltmaking from piecework.

To begin:

Look through the pages of quilt blocks in this chapter for patterns that interest you. Remember to stay away from curved seams, and from blocks with a great many pieces in them. Neither do I really advise anything too simple, such

33. *Crazy Ann*

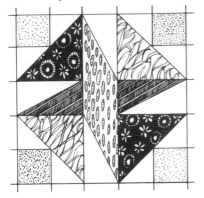

34. *Clay's Choice*

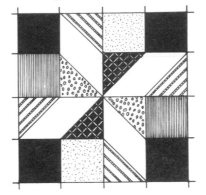

35. *Road to Oklahoma*

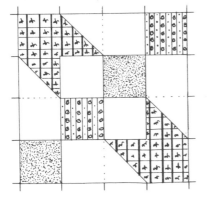

36. *Variable Star*

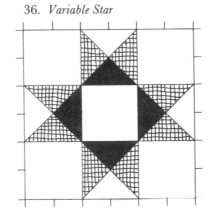

37. *Crosses and Losses*

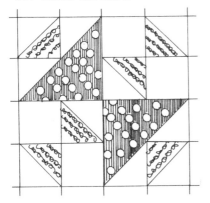

38. *Prairie Queen*

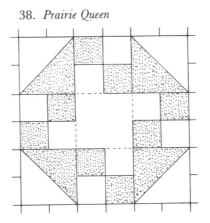

as *Checkerboards* or *Pinwheels*, in which the pattern is made entirely of a square or triangle of a single size. You will learn more if you have to make templates in a couple of different sizes and shapes, and cut and sew different kinds of pieces. On the facing page you will find six blocks that are suitable for a beginning project. You might choose one of them, or any other with a similar number and variety of pieces; just remember to go through the procedure of taking it apart in your head and reasoning through exactly how it must be sewn together to be sure it can be sewn with straight seams. (There are some patterns included here that *can* be modified for machine-sewing but are really more effective sewn in the traditional way. Sooner or later you'll probably like to try one, if only for old time's sake, but avoid them for the first project.)

DRAW THE BLOCKS ON GRAPH PAPER

When you have chosen a block or two that you are interested in, the next step is to draw them on graph paper. Don't limit yourself to one block too quickly, by the way; experiment with several at a time, making them compete with each other for your attention. Remember, the sewing is going to take a while and the quilt may last forever, so the design deserves some time too.

You'll be amazed at how many different effects you can get out of a single configuration of geometric shapes by altering colors or perhaps a line or two. Besides, this is the fun part. One night I had three women who work for an advertising agency arrive for their first quilt lesson after a ten-hour day at the office. They were very quiet for the first part of the lesson, sitting in a sort of exhausted peace among a welter of quilt books, quilts, colored pencils, rulers, and graph paper. They thumbed through books, peered at the quilts on the wall, drank their tea and giggled among themselves as they worked over several designs apiece; finally one of them said, "I can't believe you actually do this for a living—I haven't had so much fun since I was in kindergarten."

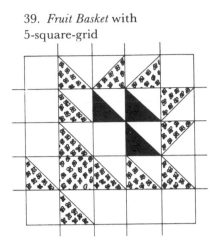

39. *Fruit Basket* with
5-square-grid

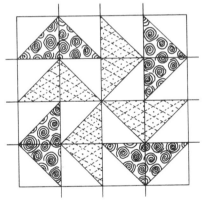

40. *Dutchman's Puzzle*

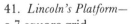

41. *Lincoln's Platform*—
a 7-square grid

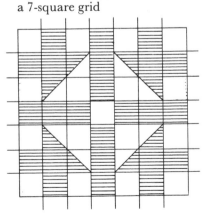

Drawing the block on paper takes the place of the old folding paper technique, and gives you a great deal more liberty with the design than the old methods; now you can alter a pattern with a stroke of a pencil instead of going through the laborious process of making a new paper block and perhaps even a sample fabric block, every time you want to test an idea. (This is another reason modern patchwork design tends to be more innovative than traditional; the old-time ladies often had little faith in their ability to create something new, and it was enormously easier to borrow somebody's templates [tracing patterns] and copy them exactly than it was to make up a new block or even alter an old one.)

To draw the block on graph paper, all you have to know is how to fit it onto a grid (graph paper is a grid). Technically this amounts to finding how many modules—measurements of equal size—the block has on each side. Some people find that explanation difficult, but that is just because this is a visual concept, not a verbal one; you do not have to know what "module" means to understand at a glance the way to draw a block on graph paper. Grids have been imposed here on some sample blocks; you can see that *Fruit Basket* has five grid squares on each side; *Dutchman's Puzzle* four, and so on. You will encounter blocks with six, seven, and nine grids; *Burgoyne Surrounded* has 17. To figure out how to reproduce them, you have to be able to use a ruler, and to count. All the blocks in this book are drawn to scale, so that if you encounter one you can't understand at a glance you can draw a grid onto it yourself and count the number of grid squares you have made.

EXPERIMENT WITH COLORS

When you first choose a block from a quilt or this book, you see it colored a certain way. It used to be that people followed each other so closely in the use of colors within a traditional block, that frequently the exact same pattern has two different

42. *Burgoyne Surrounded*

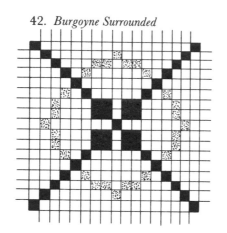

43. *Crazy Ann* outline

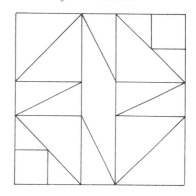

44. *Crazy Ann*: first shading

45. *Crazy Ann*: second shading

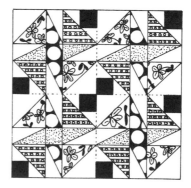

names, depending on how the lights and darks are arranged. But you should consider the arrangement of shades in each block as merely examples; changing the quality and placement of colors can change the effect of the block completely, and it is one of the most important parts of the design. When you first draw the block on graph paper, it is, of course, in outline, like the *Crazy Ann* block shown here. Using an assortment of colored pencils or nylon-tip markers (my preference), color in the block. In the first *Crazy Ann*, you see three colors used: one for the star in the center, one for the triangles, and one for the little squares. In the second version you see five colors, arranged in such a way that the eye is carried diagonally, from corner to corner, instead of focusing on the star in the center. Additionally the little squares in the top left and bottom right corners have been dropped out, so that the ones that remain give the block an even stronger diagonal bias.

DRAW FOUR BLOCKS TOGETHER

The next step is to take a block that is colored a certain way and draw it four times in a cluster, as shown, to see what patterns are created. You must always do this, for the effect of the blocks together is often far more interesting than the single block would suggest. Look at it up close, hold it away from you, and squint at it to see what kind of dance it does when reduced to black and white. Look at the drawing of the first *Crazy Ann*, drawn four together; it is simple, attractive, a little squat and four-square. Then look at the second one; it is more active, it draws the eyes this way and that instead of plunking you down in the center of each block. In addition to removing the corner squares, the colors of the center squares are alternated to match first the vertical strip, then the horizontal one. That's supposed to make the strips appear to weave over and under one another.

Even if you hit on something you like very much at this point, try at least one more block

46. *Crazy Ann*, 40″ × 50″. Author's quilt.

47. *Clay's Choice*, 32″ × 44″. Jeffrey Gutcheon's quilt.

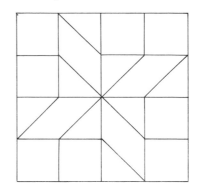

before you commit yourself. At the very least you'll learn a little more about designing patchwork, and you may hit on something really terrific. There are so many possible quilts to make, so many ways to set them together, that when you finally decide on one, it means you've decided against all the rest. Here, I've gone through the process again with *Clay's Choice,* using three colors in both experiments but having the central star appear in positive in the first and negative in the second. Finally, you can look at Figs. 46 and 47 to see *Crazy Ann* and *Clay's Choice* made up into quilts. *Crazy Ann* appears exactly as it does in the second drawing, except that it shows three blocks across and four down. *Clay's Choice* is a slightly cubist fantasy of my husband's (his first quilt).

In his *Clay's Choice,* Jeffrey has done a number of interesting things. In the first place, it was a real innovation to make the star out of the lightest color instead of the darkest. As far as I know, it's never been done before, and the block has been popular since the days of Henry Clay and for years after the memory of Clay had faded a bit when it became *Henry of the West* and finally *Star of the West.* (Which tells you not so much how clever Jeffrey is as how many new things there are for you to try.)

He has also divided all four corner squares in half diagonally, creating the extra square within a square where the corners of the blocks come together, and he has also used more than twice the usual number of colors, arranging them so that some run only from top to bottom and others only from side to side. Last, he has deliberately chosen fabrics with strong plaids or stripes and let the direction of the prints occur in a random way, trying to destroy some of the rigidly geometrical feeling of the traditional block. (Contrast this with the regular way strips are used in *Crazy Ann.*)

Remember at this point you are only dealing with placements of lines and arrangements of darks and lights; do not feel you have to indicate prints or

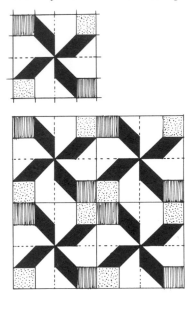

stripes or plaids in your drawing. That comes later, when you choose fabrics, and is another matter entirely. You use the colored pencils or markers only as a sort of code to yourself, indicating where different fabrics occur, and whether they are relatively dark or light.

When you have finished the drawing to your satisfaction, you have completed the design of the first project, except for the border, which is usually a plain color decided upon after the patchwork is actually completed. (You won't know what color will set off the design best until after you see the fabrics cut and sewn, nor can you really tell what width border will make the most effective frame.)

SET

Since your first project is fairly small, you can afford to use the straightforward plan of making each block patchwork, and setting them directly against one another, without intervening strips or plain blocks. This is the simplest set there is, and in most cases it is also the most dramatic. When a small child in a pioneer household became old enough to help with the work of quiltmaking, she started by helping to trace and cut and do simple sewing on her mother's patterns, but when she was allowed to plan and execute her own first quilt, she usually began with a simple square or pinwheel block, set straight together in this fashion.

LATTICE STRIPS

There are a great many other ways to set blocks together, of course. The use of lattice strips between the blocks has been very popular, especially for scrap quilts. The strips served two functions; they made the quilt top considerably larger without adding much to the work time, and they kept the blocks away from each other when the multitude of prints and colors would have clashed and jarred. The old time quiltmakers were not necessarily charmed by the randomness of scrap quilts, as we often are. To them a scrap quilt

50. *Clay's Choice:* second shading

52. *Duck's Foot*—blocks set
together

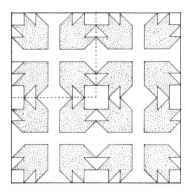

53. *Duck's Foot* with white
lattice strips

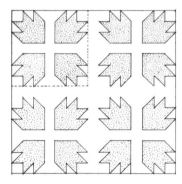

54. *Hayes' Corner* block

was a constant reminder that all their lives they would be making do, saving, scrimping, conserving. If their blocks had to be made of scraps instead of specially chosen fabrics, they at least liked the set to be neat and tidy and new.

The drawing shows the *Churn Dash* block set with lattice strips in a color contrasting with the background of the block. Another use of lattice strips is shown in the drawings of *Duck's Foot in the Mud*. In the first drawing you see the block set straight together without strips; it makes an interesting pattern, but it is a bit squat and solid. In the second drawing you see the same block separated by strips the same color as the background; suddenly the *Duck's Foot* seems to be floating. This set works well with any pattern having a strong, jagged outline. When you are experimenting with such a design on graph paper, remember to erase the pencil lines that outline the blocks after you have finished coloring. For when the quilt is made, you will hardly notice these seams and the lines on paper interfere with your ability to visualize the final effect.

ALTERNATE PLAIN BLOCKS

In Fig. 55, the *Hayes' Corner* quilt, you see another popular set: the alternate plain block. This is especially effective when the block has a strong diagonal bias; it allows the pieces to march across the background in a chain. It is also appropriate if the block has a great number of pieces in it, for if you alternate the pieced blocks with plain you obviously have only half as much work to do. Sometimes old quilts were set this way for no other reason than to give the maker plenty of blank spaces for fancy quilting.

Fig. 56, *King's Crown*, shows another diagonal pattern set with alternate plain blocks, but here the direction of the diagonals has been rearranged to make a different kind of design. In working on a design of this kind, you may find it convenient to draw and color on graph paper as many pieced

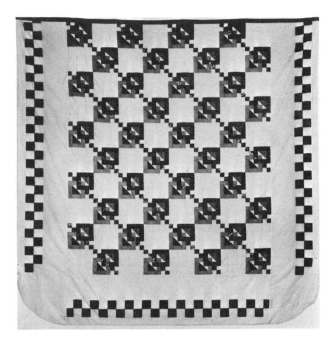

55. *Hayes' Corner* quilt, 120″ × 123″. Author's quilt.

56. *King's Crown,* 95″ × 95″. Author's quilt. Alternate plain blocks have square insets of printed Indian cotton.

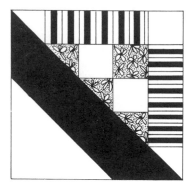

57. *King's Crown* block

blocks as you need; then cut them out and rearrange them, rather than drawing them over and over.

King's Crown is probably a very old block, for when a block was invented it was usually named for some popular hero or event of the time, in much the way the people today name their children after movie stars. Quilts were very much a part of popular culture. This block was probably named after one of the King Georges during the colonial period, or else for King David, since biblical figures were also popular heroes in Puritan New England. The block called *Queen Charlotte's Crown* was named after the wife of George the Third, last Queen of America. (Slipped your mind, didn't she?)

SETTING BLOCKS ON THE DIAGONAL

The drawing of *Union Squares* shows blocks set on the diagonal with alternating plain blocks. This is another of the patterns with a strong jagged outline that looks so effective when it is allowed to float in a plain background. (Remember to erase the pencil lines around the blocks after you finish coloring the dark parts.) The dotted lines show you how to join the blocks in diagonal strips so that it all can be done with straight seams.

STRIP QUILTS

Other patterns are always set in vertical strips instead of horizontal rows. The *Zig-Zag* or *Picket Fence* pattern shows a checkerboard scrap block set on the diagonal. (This, by the way, is the pattern I used for my famous first quilt; I took it from an old quilt bought by some friends in Bucks County, Pennsylvania, at Rice's open market, where they also go to bid on bushels of eggplants and tomatoes and the occasional live duck.)

Lightning Strips, Tree Everlasting, Tumblers, and *Delectable Mountains* are also handsome strip quilts, all of them very old patterns. *Delectable Mountains* is named after a passage from *Pilgrim's Progress,* which was the only reading matter except the Bible

58. *Union Squares:* set on the diagonal with alternate white blocks.

59. *Picket Fence* setting

60. *Lightning Strips*

61. *Tree Everlasting*

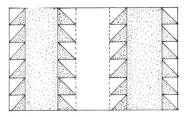

62. *Tumblers*

63. *Delectable Mountains*

73

64. *Greenberg Wedding Quilt, 92″ × 104″*. Author's quilt.

65. *Indiana Puzzle*

66. *Double Irish Chain*

67. *Double Irish Chain* blocks

in many Puritan households. Children generally learned the ABCs from it; it was considered light reading, though the Slough of Despond generally stops me cold. The *Delectable Mountain* pattern appeared later set in a block in such a way that the jagged edges appeared to whirl around like a cyclone. In that form, the pattern is called *Kansas Trouble* (shades of Dorothy and the Wizard).

TWO-BLOCK PATTERNS

Some patterns depend for their effect on two blocks rather than one. The *Greenberg Wedding Quilt* (Fig. 64) shows one of the most exciting examples. The square, which is begun in one block, is completed in the other, but this can be made very obvious or very subtle according to how you use colors. The photograph also illustrates my point about color values; the dark areas are pieced in very different fabrics, a green solid and a maroon and white print, yet they are so nearly the same in intensity of color, that in black and white they look exactly the same except for the white squiggles showing where the prints are. I took this pattern from a magazine photograph (we quilt people are notorious scavengers) of somebody's newly renovated chicken coop, or some such. A quilt in this pattern, which I have never seen elsewhere, was on the bed in the picture, but it was done in two highly contrasting colors, and looked almost completely different from this one.

Indiana Puzzle and *Irish Chain* also depend on specific alternate blocks for their effect. *Indiana Puzzle* is a popular block that is usually done with all-white alternate blocks and turkey red and called *Monkey Wrench* or *Snail's Trail.* Done as shown here with alternate white and dark solid blocks, it gives the entire pattern in positive/negative instead of one pattern on a white background.

The *Irish Chain*, a famous and beautiful pattern, requires one small colored square in each corner of the white block. These can be either set in or appliquéd on—the latter is probably easier.

69. *Greenberg Wedding Quilt* blocks

70. *Storm at Sea*

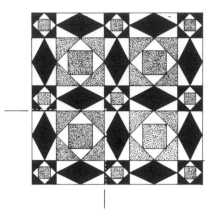

71. *Milky Way*

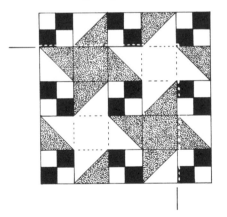

72. *Road to California*

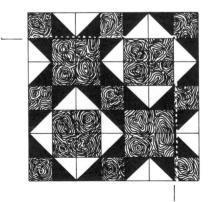

73. *Log Cabin*

74. *House*

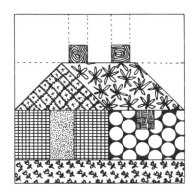

75. *Pieced Star*

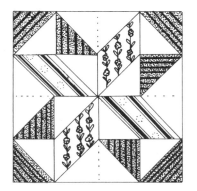

76. *Whirlwind*

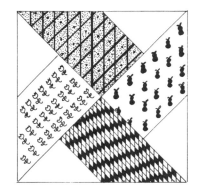

77. *Palm Leaf* or *Hosanna*

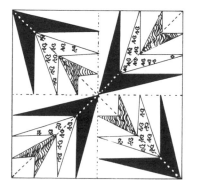

78. *String Quilt*

79. *Broken Dishes*

80. *Windmill*

81. *Wild Geese* or *Double-T*

82. *Windblown Square*

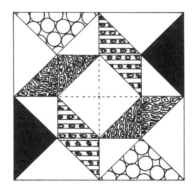

83. *Indian Hatchet*

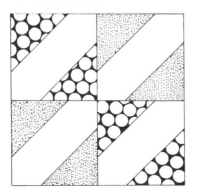

84. *Columns*

85. *Railroad Crossing*

86. *Birds in Air*

87. *Seesaw*

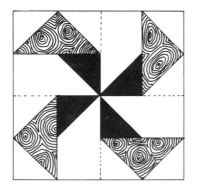

88. *Ribbons*

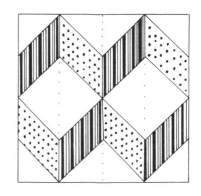

89. *Handy Andy* (1)

90. *Next Door Neighbor*

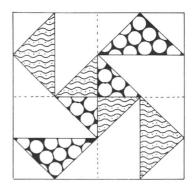

91. *Key West Star*

92. *Georgetown Circles*

93. *Flock*

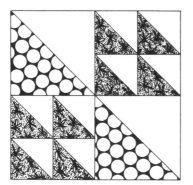

94. *Star*

95. *Maltese Cross*

96. *Small Business*

97. *Hovering Hawks*

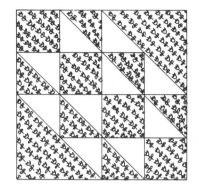

98. *Arrowheads*

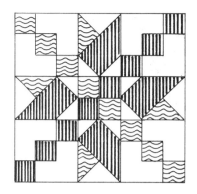

99. *Northumberland Star*

100. *Tam's Patch*

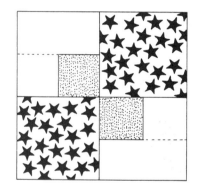

101. *World's Fair*

102. *Merry-Go-Round*

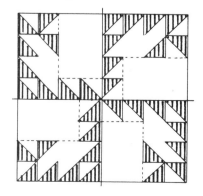

103. *Rob Peter to Pay Paul*

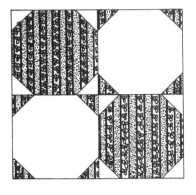

104. *Necktie*

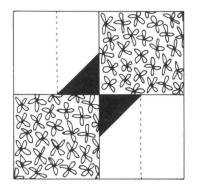

105. *Chinese Puzzle*

106. *Wild Goose Chase*

107. *Grandmother's Cross*

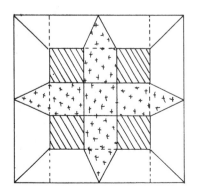

108. *Goose in the Pond*

109. *Jack in the Box*

110. *Cross and Crown*

111. *Mare's Nest*

112. *Checkerboard Skew*

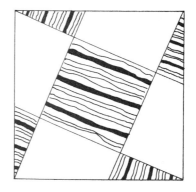

113. *Wedding Rings*

114. *Georgetown Circle*

115. *Pigeon Toes*

116. *Flying Squares*

117. *Leapfrog*

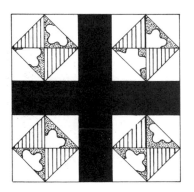

118. *Domino and Squares*

119. *Red Cross*

120. *Farmer's Daughter*

121. *Pinwheel Skew*

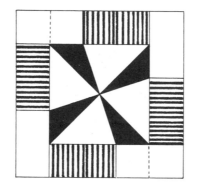

122. *Z-Cross*

123. *Tall Pine Tree*

124. *5-Patch Star*

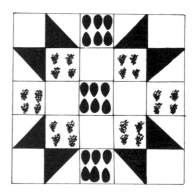

125. *Pine Tree*

126. *Sawtooth*

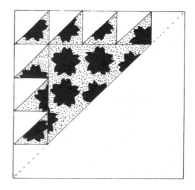

127. *Mexican Cross*

128. *Mexican Star*

129. *Grandmother's Choice*

130. *Joseph's Coat*

131. *White House Steps*

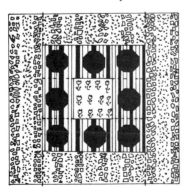

132. *Queen Charlotte's Crown*

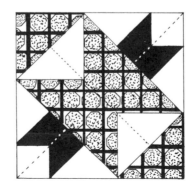

133. *Handy Andy* (2)

134. *Captain's Wheel*

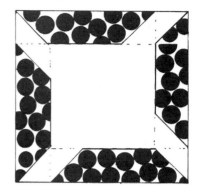

135. *Children's Delight*

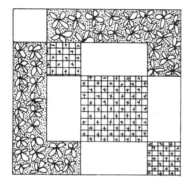

136. *Clown's Choice*

137. *Propeller*

138. *Double Sawtooth*

139. *Tea Leaf*

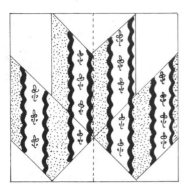

140. *Autumn Leaf*

141. *Flying Clouds*

142. *Stepping Stone*

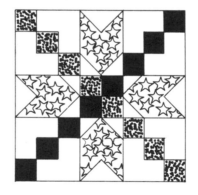

143. *Rising Star*

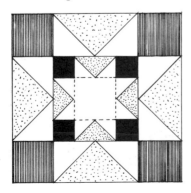

144. *8-Hands Round*

145. *Wheel of Fortune*

146. *Devil's Claws*

147. *Sherman's March*

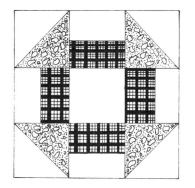

148. *Jacob's Ladder*

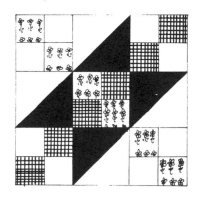

149. *Road to California*

150. *Becky's 9-Patch*

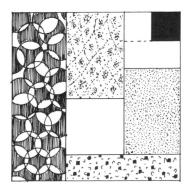

151. *Beggar's Block*

152. *9-Patch Chain*

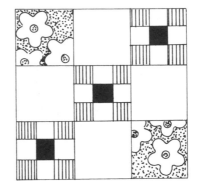

153. *Winged Square*

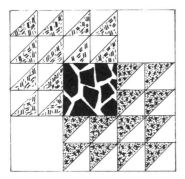

154. *Jeffrey's 9-Patch*

155. *Greek Cross*

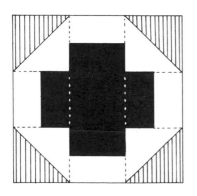

156. *Corn and Beans*

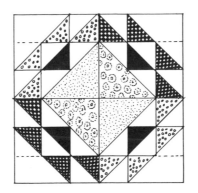

157. *Spider Web*

158. *Handy Andy* (3)

159. *Boxes*

160. *Checkerboard*

161. *Blocks and Stars*

162. *Water Wheel*

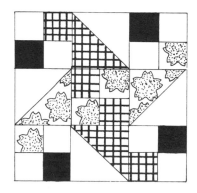

163. *Puss in the Corner*

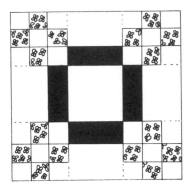

164. *Castle in Air*

165. *Domino*

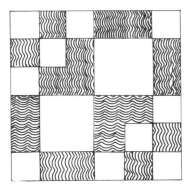

166. *Steps to the Altar*

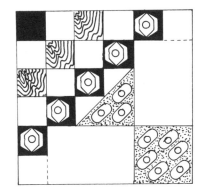

167. *Flying Dutchman*

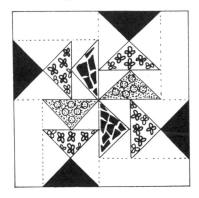

168. *Rolling Pinwheel*

169. *Bow*

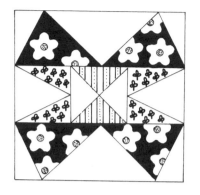

170. *Cross*

171. *Royal Star*

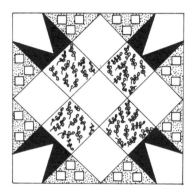

172. *Palm Leaf*

173. *Flying Bird*

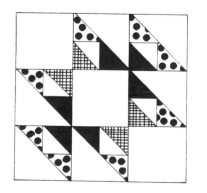

174. *Tassal Plant*

175. *Another Star*

176. *Snowball*

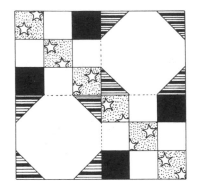

177. *54–40 or Fight*

178. *St. Louis Star*

179. *Jacob's Ladder* (oldest version)

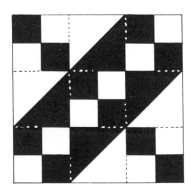

180. *Patience 9-Patch*

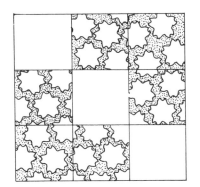

181. *Another Sawtooth*

182. *Ohio Star* or *Shoo-Fly*

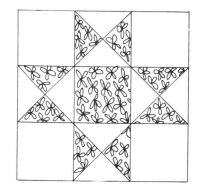

183. *Letter X*

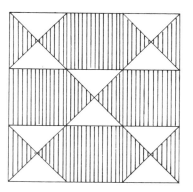

184. *Flying Dutchman* (2)

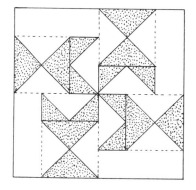

185. *Puss in the Corner* (2)

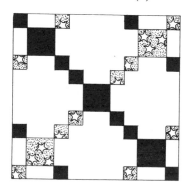

186. *Cactus Flower*

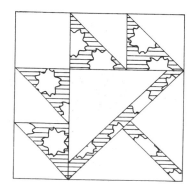

187. *Patience Corner*

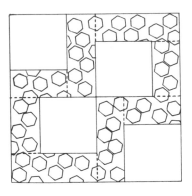

188. *Star*

189. *Cat and Mice*

190. *Union Squares*

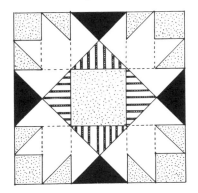

191. *8-Pointed Star*

192. *Friendship Star*

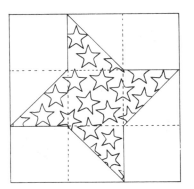

193. *Rolling Stone*

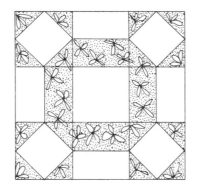

194. *Double-T*

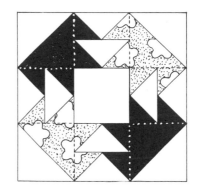

195. *Four T's*

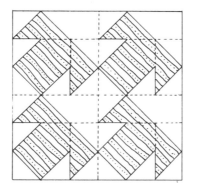

196. *Aunt Sukey's Choice* or *Puss n' Boots*

197. *Tile Puzzle*

198. *Sky Rocket*

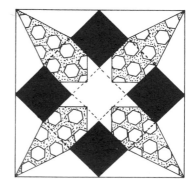

199. *Hourglass*

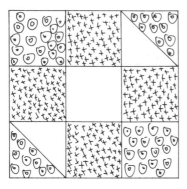

200. *Card Trick*

201. *Pinwheel Star*

202. *Spider Web* (a strip quilt)

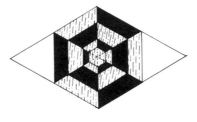

203. *Martha Washington's Star*

204. *Basket of Scraps*

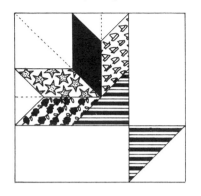

205. *Pinwheel*

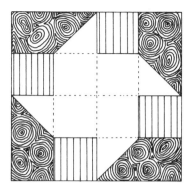

206. *Claws*

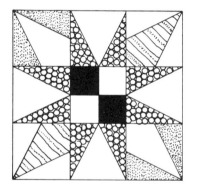

207. *Chain*

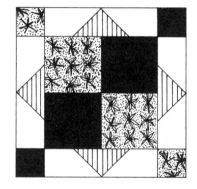

208. *V-Block*

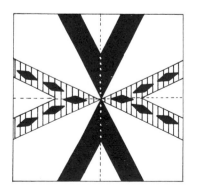

ASYMMETRICAL BLOCKS

Patterns such as *Storm at Sea, Milky Way,* and this version of the *Road to California* (which I took from a quilt in the Whitney Museum exhibit) fall into a special category. Set together, they make a regular, symmetrical pattern, but the actual design block (the unit to be repeated) is asymmetrical. You find the block by removing the border part of the design from the center pattern on two sides, as shown.

APPLIQUÉ

To design an appliqué quilt using a traditional block, you more or less follow the same train of thought as for designing a piece quilt; choose a block or two that you like, draw them on graph paper, color them different ways, draw them set in different ways until you find an effect you like. A number of blocks such as *Basket, Triple Sunflower,* and *Triangle Flower* are made using both piece work and appliqué: the regular geometric parts are pieced into the block, and the curved or irregular parts are appliquéd on afterwards. These are good choices for people who don't have much time for hand-sewing, but enjoy doing a bit of it.

Even more than piece work, traditional appliqué blocks were not so often designed as borrowed. If you wanted to make an oak leaf quilt or a *Rose of Sharon,* you sent home to your sister in Connecticut for the pattern she used, or for a sample block from which to trace a pattern. For those who are interested in reproducing a traditional pattern, borrowing is still the best technique; you can write to the Stearns and Foster Company for a catalogue of their beautiful and beautifully drawn patterns (see the list of mail-order goods and services in the back of the book). Designing piecework is essentially a graphic technique, accessible to anyone who can draw a straight line, but appliqué is essentially painterly. I can't tell you how to design it, any more than I can tell you how to draw. If you can draw well enough to reproduce

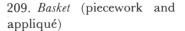

209. *Basket* (piecework and appliqué)

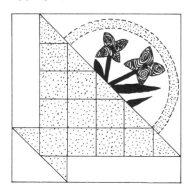

210. *Friendship Dahlia* (A)

211. *Tulip* (2) (A)

212. *Oak Leaf* (A)

213. *True Lover's Knot* (A)

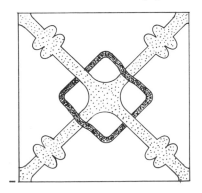

214. *Cherries* (A)

215. Paper folded in quarters

216. Cut-out pattern

on graph paper the examples of traditional appliqué blocks given here, then you don't need to borrow anyone else's pattern; on the other hand, you don't need to use a traditional pattern at all. You can draw your own, totally new, never-before-seen-on-earth pattern; virtually any line drawing can be rendered in appliqué.

If you want to invent a new appliqué block, but don't draw well enough to do one free-hand, you can try cutting designs out of paper, as you used to cut paper dolls or snowflakes in kindergarten. Fold a square of paper into quarters. As shown, draw any kind of symmetrical or asymmetrical design you like as long as you leave the two folded edges basically intact. Cut along your line and open out the paper to see what shape you have made. It's great fun; you may eventually make yourself a Rorschach blot you love and want to put on each block of the quilt or you may make 35 you like and have a different blot on each block. Or you may want to make enormous cutouts from newspaper and have only four on the entire quilt top.

You can also make a pattern for appliqué by tracing pictures from books, coloring books, photographs, or other quilts. If you plan to do this, work out the design on graph paper with colored pencils to give yourself an idea of the best placement of figures, the scale, and so on. The sketches can be very approximate—just a swiggle to indicate here a warthog, there a bird, is plenty. The tracing will be done exactly to the scale you want on the quilt, at the time you make the templates.

CURVED-SEAM BLOCKS

For those who are ready to try sewing curved seams, there are a number of simple but very exciting designs and a virtually endless number you can design yourself with graph paper and a compass.

Making a piece quilt using curved seams was such a frivolous and trendy idea that it evidently didn't occur to anyone until fairly late in the

217. *Triple Sunflower* (P & A)

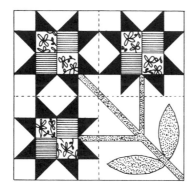

218. *Triangle Flower* (P & A)

219. *Dresden Plate* (P & A)

220. *Tulip Basket* (P & A)

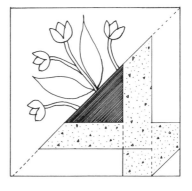

221. *Mohawk Trail* (P & A)

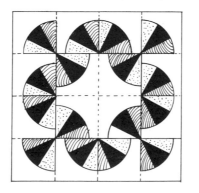

222. *Pine Tree* (P & A)

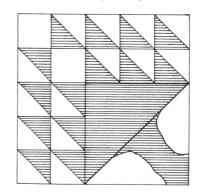

223. *Grandmother's Fan*
(P & A)

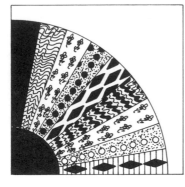

224. *Lock and Chain* (P & A)

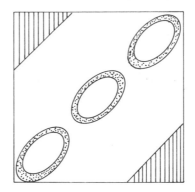

225. *Morning Star* (P & A)

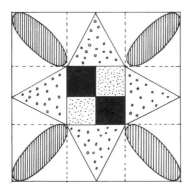

226. *Honey Bee* (P & A)

227. *Road to California* (P & A)

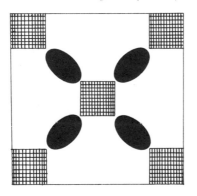

228. *North Carolina Lily*
(P & A)

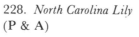
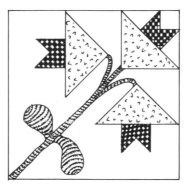

229. *Dogwood Blossom* (P & A)

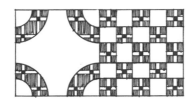

230. *Friendship Knot* (P & A)

development of the American patchwork, toward the middle or end of the 18th century. Formerly the whole point of the piece quilt was to whip something together as fast as possible to keep out the cold at night. If it was handsome, so much the better, but you couldn't go very far out of your way to make it so. The appearance of the curved seam is a good indicator of a certain change in the quilt-maker's lifestyle. Maybe she hasn't the money for fancy chintz for an appliqué quilt out of new goods, but she has a little extra time and a little more freedom to look around her and compare her life with her neighbor's, to want to do something to distinguish herself. Her quilt will probably still be made of scraps, and still be just a utility quilt, but she can at least take extra time and care with the sewing in order to do something really special and unusual.

The *Orange Peel* block is probably one of the very early curved-seam patterns. I have seen handsome versions made in the late 19th century in Bucks County, but the first one is said to have been made during the triumphant tour of the Marquis de Lafayette in colonial days. Lafayette became one of America's first pop heroes when he came to this country partly because he was a famous French general, but also because his presence indicated moral support for the struggling revolutionary forces from the glorious court of the Sun King, Louis XIV. Lafayette was petted and fêted wherever he went, and it is said that at one ball he shared an orange with a neighborhood belle, who took the curved section of orange peel home with her and made from it a patchwork pattern to remember him by.

231. *Orange Peel*

232. *Drunkard's Path*

233. *Dutch Rose*

234. *Eastern Star*

The *Drunkard's Path* block is simple in concept, if tricky to sew. A curved piece is cut out of a dark square and replaced with an identical light one; in the adjoining block a curved piece is cut from a light square and replaced with a dark one. You can draw a number of such blocks on graph paper, cut them apart, and rearrange them to make a great number of other designs.

DIAMOND PATTERNS

There are many extraordinarily beautiful patterns based on diamonds. *Baby Blocks* is a perennial favorite in Europe and America (it falls into the category of one-patch design, which must be hand-pieced, and is basically an English type of design.) American patterns include countless small diamond patterns such as *Dutch Rose, Eastern Star,* and *Doves in the Window,* and, most famous of all, the *Blazing Star* pattern, in which one enormous eight-pointed star made of tiny diamonds covers the whole quilt. These stars were also called *Lone Star, Texas Star,* or *Star of Bethlehem,* and were made in impressive numbers throughout the West during most of the 19th century.

A *Blazing Star* was the ideal masterpiece project for a pioneer woman because it was a sophisticated design problem and a challenging job of sewing, yet it was made of scraps—an important consideration to a person whose only source of new goods and supplies was the Wells Fargo wagon.

None of the diamond patterns are beginner's work, because the sides of the diamonds tend to stretch, making smooth piecing difficult. It is also more difficult to draw a true diamond pattern than some others, because it doesn't fall neatly onto a grid like the other commonly used geometric shapes. It must be constructed with each angle precisely the right size, using either a protractor, a compass, or a tracing from another perfect diamond, or the finished star will not fit together. You also have to remember the difference between diamonds and rhomboids. A rhomboid can be

235. *Electric Fans*

236. *Winding Ways*

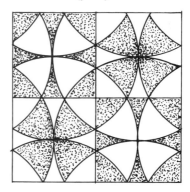

237. *Royal Cross*

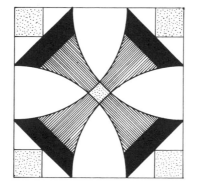

238. *Dolly Madison's Workbox*

239. *Millwheel*

drawn on graph paper easily, and some of the diamond patterns can be made using rhomboids instead of diamonds. But a rhomboid differs from a diamond in having its diagonal sides longer than its vertical ones—a diamond's sides are all equal——and using rhomboids subtly alters the effect of the pattern. Also rhomboids are only easier than diamonds on paper—drafting the templates and sewing the blocks is no more difficult with one figure than the other. For the patterns in which they are interchangeable, I advise using rhomboids during the designing stage, and changing to true diamonds when you are ready to draft the templates.

The design interest in diamond patterns comes mainly from the way in which dark and light colors are placed within each block. Some blocks can be sewn by machine, though again, it is not beginner's work. (Even the huge *Blazing Star* can be pieced on machine if an entire design is drawn out on paper first and each piece marked for color and then scrupulously followed during piecing. However, choosing precisely the right shade for each piece would take a very practiced eye.) You design a diamond quilt on graph paper as you would any other, first choosing a block, and experimenting with placements of colors, then try it set with lattice strips or alternate blocks of a solid color. These blocks often look especially handsome set on the diagonal with alternate white blocks. (See the *Union Square* set.) If you want to try that, it is definitely more efficient to cut out the blocks you have already drawn and turn them on their corners than to try to draw them on the diagonal.

QUILTS THAT DESIGN THEMSELVES

For those who prefer a more organic approach to quiltmaking there are a variety of patterns that are pieced by hand which hardly have to be planned ahead at all. *Baby Blocks, Star and Hexagon,* and *Grandmother's Flower Garden* are typical examples. They have all been very popular at one

240. *Dove in the Window*

241. *Sunburst*

242.
Rhomboid

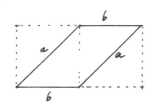

Diamond

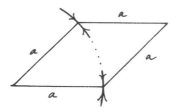

243. *Eastern Star* drawn with rhomboids

244. *Baby Blocks*

245. Grandmother's Flower Garden

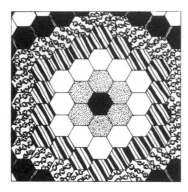

246. Star and Blocks

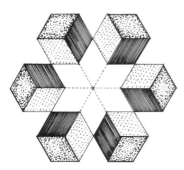

247. Star and Hexagon

time or another in the development of the American quilt, but they basically stem from the European style of patchwork and are more common in England than here. To design, you simply make a rough sketch of the basic figure and decide where you want darks, mediums, and lights. Then you separate your scraps into piles according to shade and begin to sew, choosing the color for each piece as you come to it. When you have enough *Baby Blocks*, or *Grandmother's Flowers* to make the size quilt you want, you lay them all out together and decide how to arrange them, or you can simply sew them together according to whatever order they come to hand and let the final arrangement surprise you.

BORDERS

The effect of the finished quilt depends a great deal on the right border, just as a picture requires the proper frame. Very often the best border is one or more simple bands of solid color, and if that is your plan, it is best to wait until your quilt top is entirely pieced to decide what it needs in the way of width and color. But you may prefer to plan a pieced or appliqué border as part of your design, particularly if the design is spare and simple. You can choose one of the traditional border patterns here or invent your own from some element of your pattern block. Or you can adapt the old-fashioned medallion plan, making a central area of your design relatively small, and surrounding it with 3 or 4 different border patterns. You can also use any of these borders in strips to form the entire quilt top, or in place of lattice strips between the blocks. Or use a block pattern in strips to make a border, as in Fig. 280.

ORIGINAL DESIGNS

Planning a quilt top of one or two blocks or strips to be repeated throughout is certainly the easiest design concept to handle. But you are by no means limited to that. Once you are familiar enough with construction problems so that you

248.

249.

250.

251.

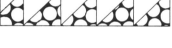

252.

253.

254.

255.

256.

257.

258.

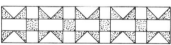

259.

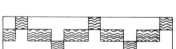

260.

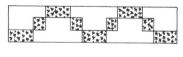

261.

262.

263.

264.

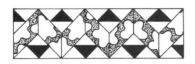

265.

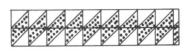

266.

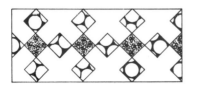

267.

268.

269.

270.

271.

272.

273.

274.

275.

276.

277.

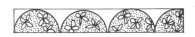

278.

279.

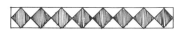

280. *Wheels*, 72″ × 72″. Author's quilt (photo: Robert Weinreb)

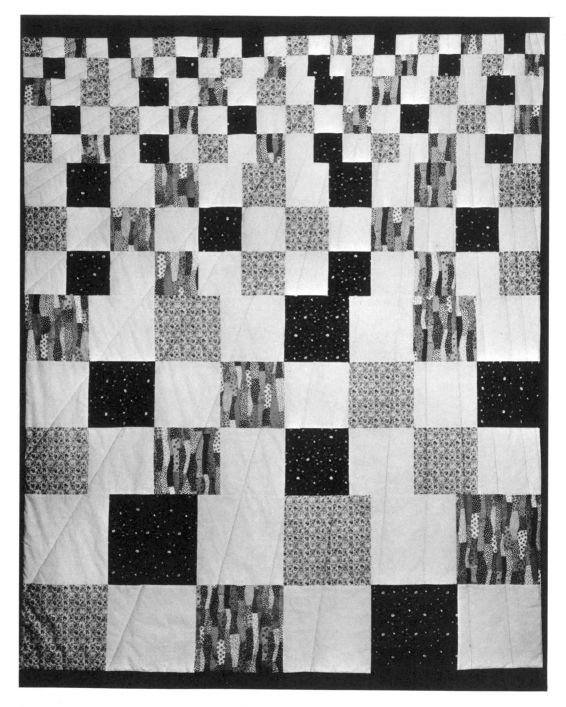

281. *Vanishing Point*, 78″ × 95″. Author's quilt.

282. *Checkerboard Skew.*

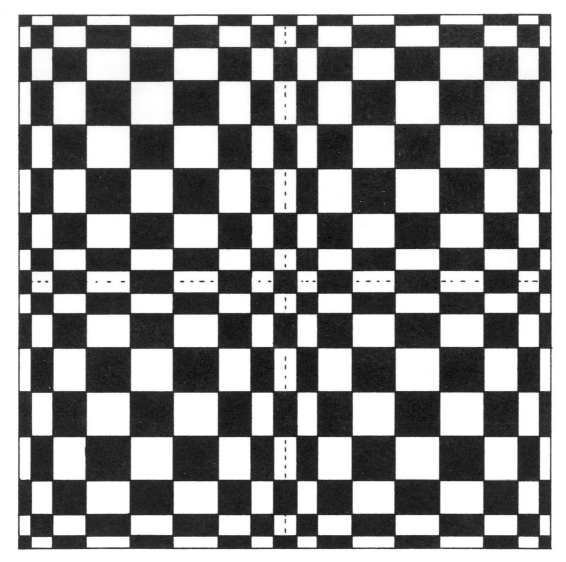

283. Op-art design from 19th-century woven coverlet

284. *Road to Oz*, 75″ × 99″. Author's quilt in gray and ochre

285. *Red and White*, 75″ × 99″. Author's quilt in two red prints

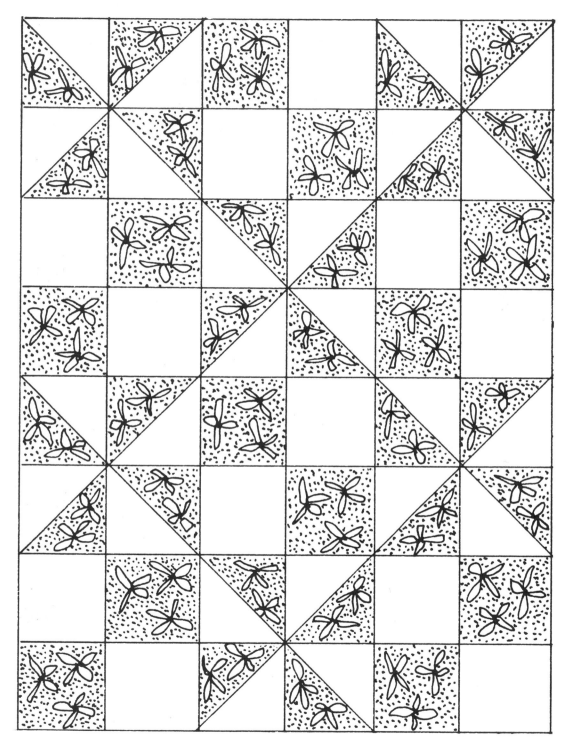

286. *Checkerboard and Pinwheels*

287. *Night and Day,* $\overline{62''} \times \overline{78''}$. Jeffrey Gutcheon's quilt, pieced in cottons and panne velvet with deep blue velvet border

don't devise something impossible to sew, you can be much more flexible about your designs. Fig. 281, *Vanishing Point,* illustrates one way to use patchwork elements in an untraditional way. Many op-art graphic effects can be adapted to patchwork, and not all of them are all that modern. The *Checkerboard Skew* design is my own, but the next drawing shows a design taken from a coverlet that was handwoven in rust and black by 19th-century Georgia slaves.

Another possibility is to cut out the pieces of the quilt top as if for a regular block pattern and rearrange them into an abstract before you sew them together. *Road to Oz* and *Red and White,* built of squares and triangles, are examples of two different designs made from exactly the same patterns. Before rearranging, the pattern looked like Fig. 286.

If you would like to try a quilt like this, draw a small design on graph paper containing the size and number of shapes you plan to rearrange. Cut out the corresponding fabric pieces and lay them out on the floor, changing and rearranging until you have the design you want. Then cut apart the paper drawing and paste the pieces to another sheet of paper rearranged to match the design you have made with fabric. Having a paper design to refer to helps you avoid confusion when you come to sew the design together.

It is also possible to create an overall design with color while keeping the pieced blocks the same. *Night and Day,* Fig. 287, modulates from rich reds, greens, and blues in the top right to almost completely washed-out yellow, ivory and white at lower left. This technique requires a complete drawing with every piece color-coded and great care in choosing the fabrics to correspond to the shading of the drawing.

Finally, you can combine different block and border elements to form overall piecework designs, such as Figs. 289 and 290.

288. On original set; *Road to Oklahoma* blocks set off-center by half the length of one block

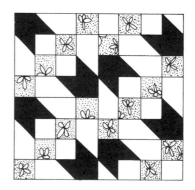

289. Overall design based on *Ribbon* and *Checkerboard* units

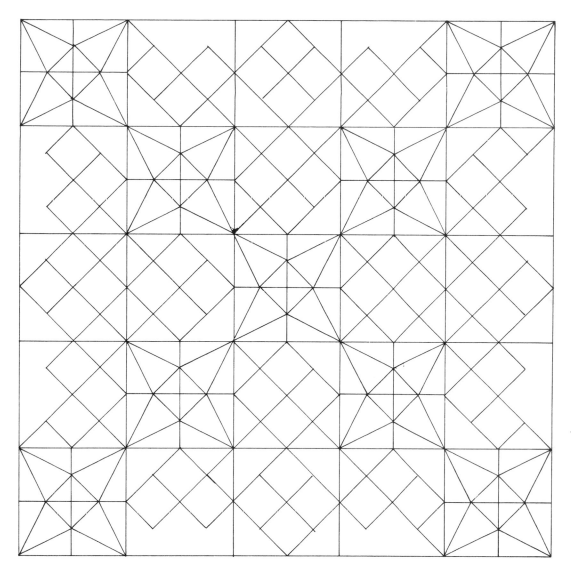

290. Overall design based on *Tippecanoe* and *Checkerboards*

6   MAKING TEMPLATES

TOOLS

After you have chosen a design and worked it out on paper, the next step is to make templates with which to trace the fabric pieces you need for the patchwork. A template is a pattern—the tissue patterns you buy for making clothes are templates of a kind—but for patchwork the template must have stiffness and thickness, because you will be tracing around it again and again and you don't want the edges to fray or the corners to be torn or rounded. In England, where people often make quilts using the same basic diamond or hexagon over and over, you can buy templates made out of plastic or plexiglass, or you might cut one from soft lead from a plumber's supply outlet. American patchworkers more usually make each quilt in a new pattern and size, and light (not corrugated) cardboard is the best medium because it is soft enough to cut with ordinary household scissors, yet it lasts as long as it needs to. I usually use posterboard from the stationery store; it is inexpensive and comes in large sheets.

DETERMINING SIZE

The size of each template will depend, obviously, on the size of the basic block you are using, and that in turn depends upon the desired size of the finished quilt top. You begin by determining the approximate size of the spread, and then figure out how many blocks of what size to use in order to arrive at that dimension. For example, if you want the finished piece to be about 70″ x 90″, you could make 10″ blocks and have the quilt 7 blocks wide and 9 blocks long. That would mean piecing 63 blocks in all. If that sounds like too much work, you could make each block 15″ square, and use only 5 across and 6 down. This would make the top 75″ x 90″, and give you only 30 blocks to piece.

THE SIZE OF THE TOP

The size of the top will depend on the size of the bed for which the quilt is made and on the way the quilt will be used. A bedspread (that is, a quilt to be used as the daytime covering for the bed) should be long enough to cover mattress, springs and pillows; a coverlet which will only be pulled up at night need not cover pillows, and a throw, which is just used over napping bodies, can be any odd size but is usually at least 4' x 4'. A baby quilt can be any convenient size between 30" and 50", smallest for a carriage blanket and larger if it is to last till the child is out of the crib. A comforter with a thick, springy stuffing should be a bit larger than a regular quilt, because it shrugs off more easily during the night, and any cover for a portly person should be larger than usual, for obvious reasons.

If possible, the best way to determine approximate size is to drape a sheet over the bed in question, folding and pinning until it looks right to you, then measure the resulting area. But if you can't or don't want to bother, you can arrive at a good size by reasoning backward from the size of the mattress. Here are the standard dimensions:

Crib—27" x 50"
Youth (cot size)—30" x 75"
Single (twin size)—39" x 75"
Double—54" x 75"
Queen—60" x 80"
King—72" x 84"

The easiest plan (and usually the most effective) is to make the area of pieced blocks about the size of the top of the mattress (less by a few inches or more by as much as a foot) and add a border or borders to fill out the top to the necessary size. For a bedspread, allow another 15" or so in length to tuck neatly around pillows. Most beds stand 22" off the floor, but old-fashioned ones may be much higher and modern ones may be lower or may not be off the floor at all, so I can't offer any exact measurements for formal to-the-floor dust ruffles. I usually aim at making the finished quilt the size of the mattress, plus 12″ to 18″ on all sides for a bedspread. That covers the pillows, mattress, and box spring (if any), and doesn't seem to fall off at night.

THE SIZE OF EACH BLOCK

It is best to be fairly flexible about the finished size of the top, because to a certain extent the size of the top is determined by the size of the blocks, and not the other way round. First you consider the scale you want for the design, which is determined by the size of the quilt and the complexity of the pattern, and to some extent by the size and style of the room for which it is made. For a full-bed quilt in an average room, 10″ to 16″ is the most effective size for a block. A block for a baby quilt should be 12″ or smaller—8″ is ideal. If you like the fine, busy look of very small pieces, feel free to make the block small, but remember that very small pieces get tricky to work with and the smaller the pieces the more there will be in the quilt top. If you are pressed for time, or don't like things too fussy-looking, or hate working on tiny pieces, you can make the block very large; a very large quilt can take a block up to 20″, but this will put the design on a very bold scale, and it would be overpowering in a small or fussy room.

The best way to determine the exact size of a single block is to decide that each grid square in your drawing of the block will be a certain dimension, and multiply. Thus, if each square of *Dutchman's Puzzle* is 2″, the whole block will be 8″ square, if each is 2½″ the block will be 10″, and if each is 3″ the block will be 12″ square. If each square of *Fruit Basket* is 2″, the block will be 10″, and so on. But if you want a *Winged Square* block 10″ square, each grid square will have to measure 1⅔″ on a side, and that creates a problem because standard measuring things (other than architect's rules) don't have thirds marked on them. In such a case

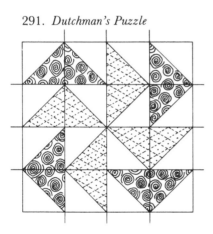

291. *Dutchman's Puzzle*

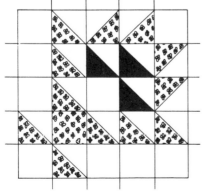

292. *Fruit Basket*

you could decide to make the block either 8″ or 12″, thus avoiding the problem, or you could construct a template ⅓″ long using a little plane geometry. (Instructions are given at the end of the chapter.)

MAKING THE TEMPLATES

Equipment: A large pad of cross-section graph paper, scissors (other than dressmaker's shears), large, clear plastic draughtsman's triangle, ruler, posterboard, double-stick Scotch Tape or glue stick, and sharp pencils.

All templates must be made extremely accurately; this cannot be overstressed. Slight variations in the size of the angles or the width of a seam margin will make the piecing tedious and difficult, and in some cases impossible. This is *not* the place to cut corners. A pad of 17″ x 22″ graph paper from an art supply store helps immeasurably; if you can get the cross-section kind which is also marked into inches, so much the better. If for any reason you have to work on unlined paper, be sure to use a draughtsman's triangle to get all the right angles as exact as possible. (You can buy a plastic triangle at art or architect's supply stores or at some stationery stores.)

OUTLINE THE PATTERN

You will need one template for each particular size and shape (not color) that occurs in your pattern. For *Checkerboard*, for instance, you need only one square; if your total block is to be 10″ square, you draft one template 5″ square, and there you are. For many blocks requiring a very few templates you can simply figure the measuring in your head and draw each one. But in a block of any complexity, the best way to avoid mistakes is simply to draw the whole block to scale and cut out the pieces you need.

For example, if you had decided to do *Crazy Ann* in 10″ blocks, you would draw the outline on

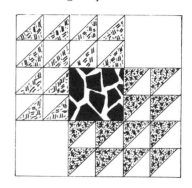

293. *Winged Square*

294. *Checkerboard*

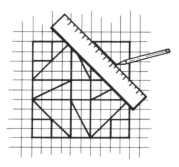

295. *Crazy Ann* being drawn

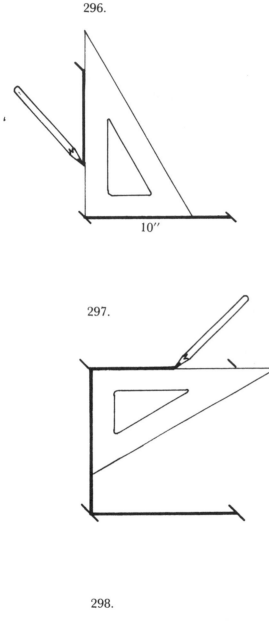

296.

10″

297.

298.

graph paper. Use a very sharp pencil, held lightly so as not to break the point, and at an angle so that the line falls as tightly as possible against the edge of the ruler or triangle. If your measurements are accurate, the horizontal and vertical lines will fall exactly on graph paper lines and the diagonals will run exactly through the corners of the grid squares. If they don't, start over.

If you are working without graph paper, use the triangle this way to outline the 10″ block:

1. First draw a straight line, then measure and mark on it two dots *exactly* 10″ apart. This is the base line of the square.

2. Place the foot of the triangle against the base line with the corner exactly at one dot; draw the perpendicular. Do the same at the other dot. This should give you three lines at perfect right angles to each other.

3. Measure and mark 10″ from the base line on each of the perpendiculars.

4. Now, the moment of truth; place the foot of the triangle against one of the perpendiculars with its corner at the 10″ mark, and draw the fourth line of the square. The line should intersect the opposite 10″ mark *exactly*. If it does not, start over; close is not close enough. If the angles are right, the sides will all be the same length. Just measure and mark off the sides of the squares into inches and draw in the seam lines of the block.

CUT OUT THE PATTERN PIECES

The next step is to cut from the block one of each of the shapes for which you need a template. Cut carefully with sharp scissors, keeping angles sharp. (Do *not* use fabric shears for this—paper dulls the blades. In fact, don't use fabric shears for anything but fabric.) Fasten each piece to posterboard, leaving plenty of room for seam margins to be added all the way around each one. Glue will do, or use double-stick Scotch Tape or a glue stick, which are less messy.

ADDING SEAM MARGINS FOR
MACHINE-SEWING

You now have patterns the size and shape of each finished piece in your block, but the template for tracing the raw pieces must obviously include seam margins outside the finished lines. Even if you have never sewn before you can see that you must not cut the fabric on the line you mean to sew.

A great controversy rages about the proper width of seam margins for patchwork. They must be wide enough that the fabrics won't ravel away from the stitches with frequent washing, but narrow enough not to leave large areas of unnecessary fabric which will interfere with quilting. Traditional quiltmakers favored ¼", and some fanatics even ⅛". I prefer ⅜", but ¼" is all right too, just as long as you're consistent. Accurate measuring is important here, for the margin edge determines the seam line in machine-sewing. The raw edge of the fabric is fed against a line on the throat plate exactly ⅜" (or ⅝" in dressmaking) from the needle. So if the width of the margin is wrong, the line of sewing will fall in the wrong place, and in patchwork every little error counts. This method eliminates the need for making a mark on the fabric exactly on the seam line, which might show through later. Most machines have these margin lines engraved on the throat plate beside the needle, but if yours does not, make your own mark by placing a finished template in the machine as if it were fabric. Lower the needle until it rests exactly at the seam line, then stick a strip of masking tape on the throat plate along the outside edge of the posterboard.

To draw the seam margins, you first draw a series of dots ⅜" (or ¼") outside the edge all around each piece. Be sure to hold the ruler perpendicular to the line during this process—any variation will change the measurement. Then connect the dots, using a ruler or other straight edge.

This process is much simplified by a thing called a Dressmaker's T-square, which has two

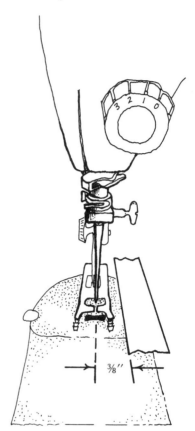

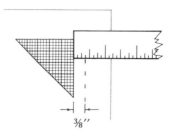

300.

301. Dressmaker's T-square

right angles to help you make sure that your corners are perfectly square. It is transparent, and is printed with an ⅛″ grid. This allows you to position the edge of the T-square ⅜″ outside the edge of the pattern without bothering with little dots, so you can just trace along the side of it. Again, when drawing margins be sure to hold the pencil lightly and at an angle, and to keep it sharp. Transparent tools, the triangle or the T-square, are always a help in getting the line to fall exactly where you want it.

WINDOW TEMPLATES FOR HAND-SEWING

A template for hand-sewing differs from one for machine-sewing in that it must allow you to mark exactly on the seam line so you will know where to sew. In the old days a template was made without margins; one traced around it on the fabric, spacing the pieces to allow for margins, and then cut a bit outside the line leaving margins as even as possible by eye. This made for some wasted fabric, but it was fairly satisfactory because a person who had been making patchwork since the age of three soon learned the difference between ¼″ and ⅜″. A less acute judge of small distances is best advised to take a little extra trouble.

Once you have made your templates as you would for hand-sewing, and have cut them out, you can make them into window templates by cutting out the center along the seam lines with a sharp scissor or a utility knife. You can then draw the cutting line on the fabric around the outside of the template and the seam line around the inside. This is an especially good device if you plan to sew part by machine and part by hand, for if you start the old-fashioned way with inexact margins and want to switch to machine in the middle, you're up the creek. If the window template is to be large, and may prove to be too flimsy, cut spaces along the seam line as shown, leaving some of the middle in place to brace the edges.

302. Using a window template

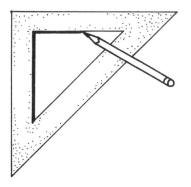

303. Large window template

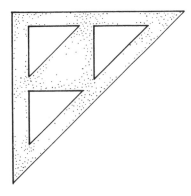

DIAMOND AND HEXAGON TEMPLATES

Diamonds and hexagons (and pentagons, which are used in small patchwork objects other than quilts) cannot easily be drawn on graph paper with just a ruler. For these shapes you have to be able to draw angles of odd sizes, which can be done with a compass if you know plane geometry, or with a protractor, or by tracing a drawing having angles the correct size as is suggested here.

Two species of diamond are commonly used in patchwork. The 45°-135° diamond makes an 8-pointed star, and is used in such figures as *Eastern Star* and *Dove in the Window.* It can be machine-pieced and the template should be made with measured margins. When you draw a block with an 8-pointed star, you reverse the usual procedure for drawing the full-size block. First make a paper diamond in a reasonable size without seam margins, and draw the pattern from the center of the block outward by tracing around the paper pattern. Add the outline of the square last.

A 60°–120° diamond makes a 6-pointed star and appears as *Baby's Blocks, Star and Blocks,* or *Star and Hexagon,* depending on how you color and set it. The hexagon in *Grandmother's Garden* and assorted mosaics is a 6-sided figure with all sides even and all angles 120°.

The three figures here give you the necessary angles exactly. To construct them in the size you need, take a tracing of these angles with tracing paper or any paper that is the least bit transparent (graph paper is fine). Put the tracing over posterboard with a piece of carbon paper underneath the tracing, and draw over the angles again to transfer them to the posterboard. Cut out a template of the two angles. Then make a figure of any size you want by drawing an angle with the template, extend the line to the proper length, add the next angle with the template, and so on.

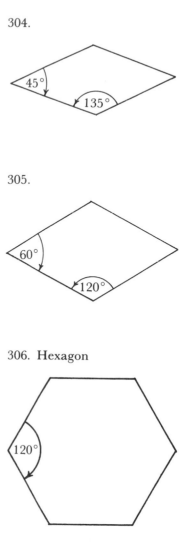

304.

305.

306. Hexagon

307. Using a traced template to make a larger template

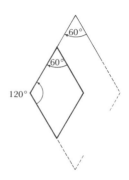

308. Small figure traced on graph paper

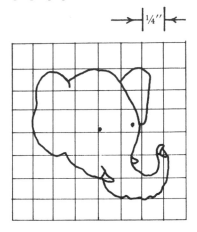

309. Figure enlarged

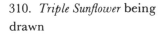

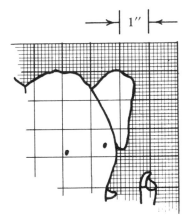

310. *Triple Sunflower* being drawn

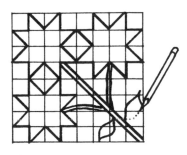

APPLIQUÉ TEMPLATES

Templates for appliqué are made to the exact size and shape of the finished piece, without margins. The patterns are traced onto the fabric directly on the seam line and a margin is left outside the line during cutting. Shapes for templates are often taken with the tracing technique described above. For example, you could make a child's quilt with characters from her favorite books by tracing the pictures on tracing paper, then transferring the tracing to posterboard with carbon paper. (If the figure is to be used only once, transfer it directly to the fabric using dressmaker's carbon paper.) Coloring books are also easy to trace, or you can draw the figure completely freehand on paper and transfer it to posterboard in the same way. If you trace a small picture or photograph on graph paper you can then enlarge the figure by making a larger grid and carefully drawing in the larger squares what you have traced in each small one.

BLOCKS COMBINING PIECEWORK AND APPLIQUÉ

For a block like *Triple Sunflower*:

1. First outline the block on graph paper and draw in the pieced areas of the design as usual.

2. Draw in the stems and leaves freehand. Take care not to make the stems too narrow; remember you will have to tuck seam margins underneath.

3. Transfer the outlines of each appliqué piece to posterboard with carbon paper; then cut out the piecework patterns and construct their templates on posterboard with margins for machine-sewing.

The templates for the portions to be appliquéd are cut out along the lines that will form the finished edge of the fabric; during cutting leave a small amount of margins for turning under.

TEMPLATES FOR CURVED SEAMS

There is no useful rule of thumb for making the patterns based on arcs. Each is different and must be worked out its own way. In each case, the difficulty lies in discovering the center of the circle of which the arc is a part, and for this, graph paper is helpful.

Sketch the pattern on graph paper as accurately as you can—freehand. Then with a compass try to duplicate what you have drawn. If you succeed, you can count the number of squares the point of the compass is from the arc, and once you know that dimension you can draw the figure to any scale you wish by multiplying. If that's too complicated, approximate the pattern using whatever readymade arcs you have around the house, such as dinner plates or teacups. This will limit your control over the size of the arcs and may alter the pattern from what you see in the book but who knows—you may like the new pattern better.

If you need to make an arc bigger than the reach of your compass or your dinner plate, tie a string around a pencil close to the point and use this device as a compass with the taut string held down where the point of the compass would ordinarily be.

CONSTRUCTING ⅓″

Last and probably least, here is a way to make a template ⅓″ long in case you need to measure thirds.

1. First, draw line A, exactly one inch long.

2. Using your triangle, draw line B above and line C below, as shown. It doesn't matter what angle you make as long as they're exactly the same. Make sure the base of the triangle is even with line A and that the point is tight at the 1″ mark. Lines B and C will be parallel.

3. Then measure the same two spaces—say ¼″ or ⅜″ long—on lines B and C. Connect the dots as shown. Line A will be divided into thirds.

311.

A

312.

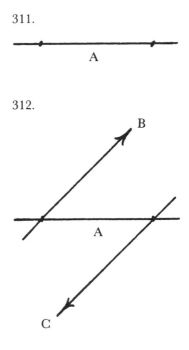

313. Line A trisected

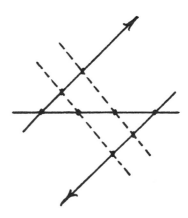

7 FABRICS

CALCULATING THE AMOUNT

After you have made all your templates, the next step is to choose the fabric. You have already determined how many fabrics you need, and you have marked on your design where and how often each fabric occurs, but these are indicated on your drawing only by different colors of ink or pencil. Before you go to choose the actual fabrics to correspond with each color on the drawing, you must figure out exactly how much of each you need. You don't want to waste a lot of money by buying more than you need, but even more important, you must not buy less than you need. It's easy to say, "Oh, I won't bother, I'll just buy ten yards of everything," but often you find a remnant on the end of the bolt that is exactly what you want. When there is no possibility of getting more, you must know exactly how much is enough.

To do this, you must make yourself a chart showing the shape and color of each kind of piece in the quilt, and beside it the number of times it occurs in the entire top. Then, using the templates you have made, you figure out the amount of yardage required for each piece. The chart for the *Crazy Ann* baby quilt, Fig. 46 (page 65), is given here. It shows a picture of each piece, and beside it the number of time the piece occurs in the block, multiplied by the number of blocks (twelve) in the quilt.

Next figure the amount of fabric you need for each piece of a kind. Most goods suitable for quilts these days come in 45″ widths, so use any 45″ piece of fabric, or tape two marks 45″ apart on a table to represent a width of fabric. Take the first template and lay it out between the marks as if for cutting, to see how many can be cut from one row of fabric. The large dark triangle would go like this.

Suppose you found that you could cut 14 triangles from one row of fabric. You need 24 in all,

314. *Crazy Ann* blocks

134

because there are two in each block and twelve blocks in the top. You would need two full rows of 14 each to get 24 triangles, and you would have a little extra.

If the triangle template is about 4¾" high (as it was in this case, being 4" on a side plus ⅜" seam margins), consider the row 5" high to give yourself breathing room. Never calculate to the last millimeter. You need 2 rows 5" high, so you indicate on the chart beside the dark triangle that you need at least 10" of dark fabric for that piece.

Next you observe that there is a white triangle in the design the same size as the dark one which also occurs twice in each block. You mark on the chart beside the white triangle that you also need 10" for that piece. Do the same for the large print triangle which is used twice in each block.

Fill out the amounts needed for each piece on the chart, then add the amounts needed for different-shaped pieces of the same color. For example, here there are three different amounts of white called for; you add them and buy a single piece of fabric large enough to supply all three. Take the chart with you when you shop, and if you possibly can, buy a little extra of each color. At the very least you will someday have a fine collection of remnants for a scrap quilt, but this will also give you the extra space you may need to cut the patterns in special ways. If the fabric is striped, you may want to cut in such a way that the stripes will run in different directions, or if it is boldly printed you may want to space the pieces so as to center the most effective parts of the print. Also, remember to buy extra fabric if the bolt is less than 45" wide.

If you would rather work out fabric requirements mathematically than empirically, there is a simple formula, provided you remember some high-school geometry and can multiply fractions. To figure how much fabric you need for a given piece, find the area of the template (including seam margins), multiply by the number of pieces, and divide by the width of the fabric. Since

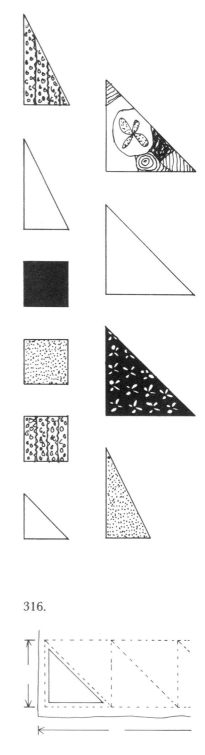

315. Piece chart

316.

135

any given patchwork shape is not likely to fit the fabric width exactly when laid out for cutting, add a conservative ten percent to your answer and round off to the nearest larger half-yard or yard. The only real kicker in this is finding the area of things like rhomboids. It seems very tricky to me, but then I have trouble balancing my checkbook. If you have a head for figures and an old geometry text around, you might really enjoy the exercise. Again, the formula is:

$$\frac{\text{Area of piece (square inches)} \times \text{number of pieces}}{\text{fabric width (inches)}} = \text{length needed}$$

LATTICE STRIPS

If the quilt is to include lattice strips, you must figure the amount of fabric you need for them, too. If the *Crazy Ann* baby quilt were to be set with 2″ lattice strips, it would be constructed as shown, with 8 vertical strips the length of one block and 3 horizontal strips the length of 3 blocks plus 2 strips.

Each block is 10″ plus ⅜″ margins on all sides, so you would need 8 strips 10¾″ long. Four of these strips laid end to end could be cut from one 45″ width of fabric. Since each raw strip is 2¾″ wide, you would need about 6″ of material for 8 vertical strips.

The horizontal strips would then be 34¾″ long (10″ for each block, 2″ for each strip, plus ⅜″ margin on each end), so you would need another 3″ of fabric for each one. Total: 15″ for strips. Again, you should get a bit extra if you can.

For any quilt whose finished width is greater than 45″, you have an additional problem; the horizontal strips will have to be pieced (sewn from smaller pieces) to span the quilt. If you don't care where the seam falls, this won't matter, but if you want the seam in the center, remember to account for this when you figure your fabric requirements.

317.

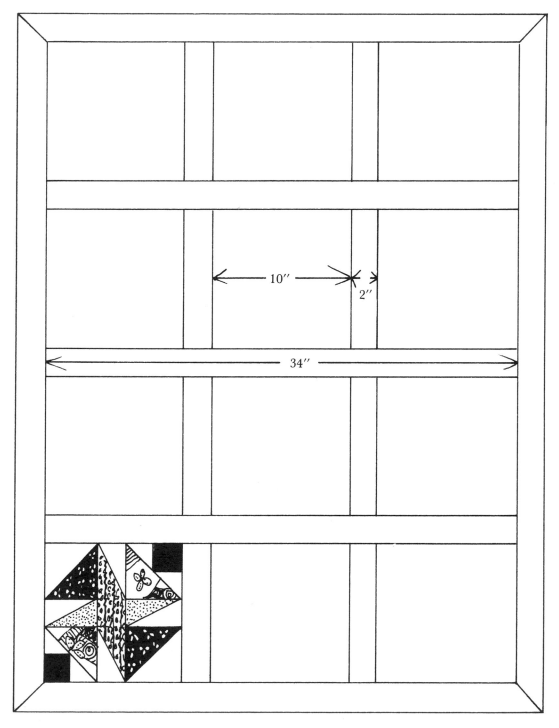

BACKING

You may want to buy backing fabric at the same time that you buy the rest of the material, particularly if it is to be patterned, or coordinated with the patchwork in some way. For a baby quilt like *Crazy Ann*, in which the area to be backed is narrower than the width of the backing material, you need only a length of fabric as long as the quilt. If the top is wider than 45″, you usually buy two pieces of fabric the length of the quilt and seam them together side by side. When you come to assemble the quilt you center the top so that the seam on the back runs down the middle of the quilt and trim as much as necessary from each side. This wastes some fabric, but backing material is inexpensive and you can always use the extra in other patchwork. You can even make the back first and use the trimmed edges in this quilt top, especially if you use white muslin.

BUYING FABRIC

Except for crazy quilts and an occasional woolen scrap quilt, traditional patchwork was made of cotton; first it was chintz, then calico. Colors went in and out of fashion; green was very popular in the early 19th century when they found the first true green dye, and later Turkey Red, which was bright and fairly colorfast, enjoyed a vogue, though no truly colorfast red was found until after World War II. Browns and blacks were the thing during the Civil War. But throughout, the staple was calico—brightly colored printed fabrics which gradually faded to the charming and muted colors we associate with old quilts today.

Fortunately or unfortunately, the textile trades have taken several giant steps in the last few decades. Most colors are quite fast (though you must still be careful of some imports). This means much less danger of colors running into each other when you wash, but it also means that you can't buy bright colors and expect them to fade and tone down after washing; they won't, at least not for a long time. (If you really want to fade colors, try washing them in hot water and chlorine bleach.)

Another modern difficulty is knowing when to use synthetics and fabrics with no-iron or permanent press finishes. Ideally, quilt fabrics should be dress or shirt weight. Synthetic crepes and knits, like Banlon, are far too sheer or stretchy, though they may be very strong. (If the fabric stretches, you will have trouble piecing it; if the cutting marks and seam margins show through a sheer fabric they will spoil the effect of the patchwork.)

Permanent press fabrics sometimes shrink badly, and many have a stiff, shiny finish that makes quilting difficult. Old-fashioned calico prints are often reproduced on permanent press sailcloth, which is almost as heavy as denim, and much too heavy for quilting. Remember that you will be trying to make small, even stitches through two layers of fabric and one of batting, or as many as six layers when you cross-seam margins. Stiff, heavy fabric would force you to take long stitches one at a time, or they might bend or break the needle.

If you are deliberately seeking a contemporary effect you can use corduroys and velveteens of the lightest weight. You should test carefully for color-fastness and shrinking, and not plan on very delicate quilting. But be aware that it is fairly tricky to use fabrics with a nap or pile (a downy or fuzzy surface) together with smooth fabrics. The nap tends to shift and skid, and requires more basting than is normally necessary. (Two fabrics with nap tend to grip each other and, except for velvets, are easy to work with.

Silks and velvets are, of course, only for quilts that need not be washed, and on the whole, a quilt top with very different weights and textures will not be quilted. (Different weights force you to take a different length of quilting stitch on each piece, which looks strange. So if you choose silks and velvets be aware that you are limiting yourself. You should also keep in mind that silks and velvets show a hole from every pin and needle you use, so they must be basted with great care, if at all. (A problem, because velvet against silk is the shiftiest, slipperiest combination of all. In any case, these fabrics are not for novices.)

The ideal patchwork material is still cotton, or a blend of dacron or rayon and cotton. Be sure to read the labels on the end of the bolt for fiber content, and to finger the material; at the very least you will also learn quickly to tell a great deal about the fabric from the way it feels. It should seem like something to use to make a shirt or blouse; if you can conceive of using it for a child's trousers, it is probably too heavy. Prints should be very small, except for special effects. Large prints tend to look blotchy when cut into small pieces. Remember, too, that the effect of the fabrics combined is far more important than any single fabric. Fairly often people look at my quilts and say, "How did you know such an ugly material would look so nice in a quilt? I wouldn't be caught dead wearing it." Then they cover their mouths and look embarrassed, and I'm always pleased. I usually wouldn't be caught dead in it either, but one of the most important parts of the craft (certainly the hardest to teach) is to choose fabrics that will blend well and show to advantage when cut in little bits.

A friend of mine who went to India last year was so thrilled with the color and crush of the market places that she hauled home three bolts of sari material, planning to drift around West 81st Street in them. But when she got home she found that they were each rather dull and disappointing, and she realized that the saris were beautiful in a crowded Eastern street because there were hundreds of them, all different and all in motion, but individually they were frankly undistinguished. The same is often true of quilting fabrics. So choose carefully and don't be rushed. Try not to shop at busy hours because the salespeople won't appreciate your blocking the aisles and wasting their time with your pondering. If you have to make two trips or go from store to store, carry swatches with you. Don't try to test combinations from memory and try not to buy one fabric until you have decided on all. After a while, if you plan to go on making quilts, you will probably start keeping an eye out for likely patchwork fabrics and buy a couple of yards every time you see a good one. When you have an assortment of materials, all of which you like, you can choose the combinations at home at your leisure, which is the best possible situation.

You may have trouble buying cottons out of season. If the department stores are featuring only tweeds for fall, try remnant stores—stores that buy ends of bolts from clothing manufacturers and fabric mills. Most small neighborhood fabric stores carry remnants, but many also carry seconds—be sure you know the difference. A remnant is a perfectly good, but short, length of fabric left on the bolt. A second has something wrong with it, such as bad printing, defective weave, or holes in it, footprints on it, or dry rot. Very often seconds are perfectly good to a quiltmaker, who can cut around the defects, and they are always inexpensive unless the store owner is a crook. Don't avoid seconds, but be careful.

Locating solid color cottons is another seasonal problem. Most big stores have a limited selection during the period the fashion industry dictates we should be stitching away on our "cruisewear" wardrobes. But from September to January they seem to vanish, and all you can find is cotton or synthetic lining materials, which are too sheer. Again, the best places to shop are neighborhood remnant and seconds stores. But wherever you look, be especially alert about the weight of a solid color fabric. Remember when you shop for quilting fabrics that you are shopping for what the textile industry thinks of as "home dressmaking" fabric. This means that if they think you don't want to wear it, you aren't going to find it, and for the moment anyway they think we only want solid colors to line our printed clothes.

Hardest of all to find is a pure white. If you ask for bleached muslin you will often be offered a lining material, or linen suitable for tablecloths or sheets. The fabric must be light, but opaque, so that the margins and cutting marks on the back of the patchwork don't show through the top too much (a greater problem with white than any other color). If you prefer blue-white to off-white, the best alternative may well be to buy permanent press sheets. (Regular sheets are not good—even cut into bits and sewn into patchwork they look exactly like wrinkled old sheets.) Percale is the right weight but it is so tightly woven that it is harder to quilt than muslin. I avoid the problem by using unbleached muslin, which is stronger than bleached and readily available, and which I happen to like better anyway. You may want to buy it by the pound. A neighborhood remnant store may sell it this way, or you can look up a wholesale piece-goods dealer in the yellow pages. It costs about 65¢ a pound—a pound being about three yards. A wholesaler probably won't want to cut a piece for you, but you can usually paw around and find one weighing three or four pounds. In addition to saving money, it saves bother to have a lot on hand because you don't have to work out how much fabric you need to buy for white pieces or white strips or backing.

Be sure not to pay too much for any fabric for patchwork, particularly if you are interested in a traditional look. American patchwork was invented for economy, and though it quickly became something more, it never became something else. If it ceases to be economical, it ceases to be real patchwork. Even the Victorian crazy quilts, which from one point of view seem an expensive parody of the early colonial crazy quilt, were conceived to avoid wasting costly silk and velvet scraps from the cutting table. Real patchwork has a spirit as well as a form, and if you violate the spirit completely, even while observing the form, you may or may not end up with a handsome bedspread, but it won't be much like patchwork.

The principle of observing the spirit of the tradition holds true in making a scrap quilt. If you set out to buy 34 fabrics, one-eighth of a yard apiece, hoping it will look as if you'd collected scraps for years, you will a) probably drive the storekeeper bunkers and b) probably wind up with a quilt that looks as if you'd gone out to buy scraps you're pretending you collected. Prints and colors are affected by fashions like everything else; even if you don't know *how* you know, you will know that a given bunch of fabrics are all the taste of one person in one year. Quilts are dated by the way their prints and dyes reflect the fashion of the times; in the 1820s it was all green flowers and fragile birds, and in the 1930s it was all art-deco amoebas, and in the 1970s it is something else. I don't mean that you won't make a perfectly handsome quilt with an artificial scrap collection; you probably will. But if it happens you want it to look like a real scrap quilt, try to get some real scraps. Cut up your old clothes, get scraps from your friends, or buy some old shirts and blouses at second-hand stores and rummage sales.

Naturally, there are exceptions to the principle that patchwork fabrics are inexpensive. Some imported cottons, particularly English and Swiss, are very expensive and are ideal in patchwork. But be wary of such expensive imports as those from India (madras or otherwise), Africa and Finland (such as Marimekko). They come in gorgeous prints, usually too large for conventional patchwork but perfect for a bold contemporary approach. However, many of them run badly—sometimes because of inferior dyes, sometimes by design. In a single garment, entirely printed in deep colors, the slight running and fading that occurs with washing may enhance the charm of the whole, but in a quilt top when the dark colors start leaking all over the lights and whites, you have a mess.

When you pay a high price for fabric you may really be paying for the no-iron finish or the sizing, or the fact that it handles and wears like canvas. All these are great advantages if you are making children's overalls, but a pure liability in a quilt.

PREPARING FABRICS FOR PATCHWORK

Before you begin to cut and sew you should preshrink all fabrics by washing them in warm water, and test them for colorfastness, no matter what they say on the label. If ever I ignore my own advice and buy fabric with a no-iron finish, I usually wash it once in hot water with bleach to destroy the stiffness and sheen, and to shrink it. A little fading is fine with me, but stiffness could interfere with quilting, and shrinking can pucker or tear the patchwork (if some pieces shrink and others don't).

Test fabric for colorfastness by putting a swatch in a bowl of warm water. Leave it for at least an hour, and swish it around once in a while to see if the water begins to change color. If the dye runs, the home remedy is to cook the fabric on the stove in a pot of water and a few tablespoons of vinegar, then wash it with something white. The vinegar should set the dye, but if it hasn't the something white will show it. You can then wash it a million times until it stops running (i.e. until the white thing stays white) or better yet, don't use it.

One last word of caution. Some dyes are perfectly colorfast when washed but react badly to the chemicals used in dry cleaning. You must be particularly careful about these if the quilt you are making is very large and will not fit into a washing machine. Beware of fabrics labeled Do Not Dry Clean, just as you avoid those for Dry Clean Only or Hand Washable. Unfortunately the worst offenders will probably not be labeled and the sales person may not know the fabric's properties. The only trouble of this kind I've had was with a scarlet African cotton. This may be too narrow a warning or too broad, but if there's a chance the quilt may be dry-cleaned, I'd be very careful of African or Indian or Finnish cottons in red or purple, for these are the touchiest dyes, or of any cotton whose origin I didn't know.

8 CONSTRUCTION

Tools: Sharp pencil, sharp scissors, washable-ink nylon-tip markers, marking chalk, iron, pins, needle, and thread and or sewing machine.

IRONING: CARING FOR AN IRON

Fabrics should be freshly pressed before they are marked for cutting. If you don't have an ironing board you can use a towel on a table, since the work is all flatwork, but you must have a good iron Steam is the best, but if you don't have it, keep a spray bottle of water handy for stubborn creases. Any empty spray-cleaner bottle is ideal. Be sure to iron at the proper heat for the fabric; synthetics take a lower heat than cotton and if ironed too hot they melt and gum up the soleplate. (That's an additional reason for ironing everything well before you make the quilt; after it is pieced you have to iron cool enough for the most sensitive fabric and that may not be hot enough for the pure cottons.)

If you should gum up the soleplate, clean it at once or it may stick or scorch or stain other fabrics. Run the hot iron over waxed paper, then scour it with fine steel wool. Scouring removes the finish on the soleplate, but you can get a spray can of stuff to replace it at housewares stores or from the manufacturer of the iron. If you live in a hard-water area, you should also get some demineralizing crystals for a steam iron; otherwise mineral deposits build up in the tank and around the steamholes and soon you are staining fabrics and scouring the soleplate again. Distilled water is not demineralized; look for crystals at housewares stores or large supermarkets.

PREPARING SCRAPS

Scraps from the cutting table should be washed to preshrink them and tested for colorfastness as are new fabrics. Old clothes need not be washed, but they should be well ironed. When you cut old clothes apart, don't bother to delicately rip seams to save every little bit of fabric; the holes from the old line of sewing will show even if you remove the thread, and the margins often have not faded with the outside of the garment and will thus be unusable because they are quite a different color. Just cut ½″ or so on either side of each seam and discard the seam area. Similarly, cut off and discard pockets, cuffs, yokes, collars, and any other place where the fabric is doubled. If you tried to save them, you would find the outside folds frayed or stained, the inside of the fold furry with lint, and the fabric unevenly faded. It is much more trouble than it's worth. Press all pieces well, and be sure to cut around stains, holes and areas weakened by wear. Avoid the whole garment if a part is *badly* worn; no quilt of used fabrics can last as long as one from new, but it really outghtn't to disintegrate on the first washing.

MARKING FOR MACHINE-SEWING

Because the exact size of each piece is so important in patchwork, each piece must be separately traced and cut. To begin, lay the first template against the selvedge (edge) on the wrong side and trace around it with a nylon-tip pen. These are much better for this purpose than pencils, which were usually used, because they don't lose their points, they show up better, and you don't have to use any pressure on the fabric to make a mark. But be sure the pen has a fine point, because you don't want a fat, sloppy mark that might throw off your measurements and show through the quilt top. Flairs or Pentels from dime or stationery stores are fine. They should have washable ink; you can test this by making a mark on your hand, then wet your finger and rub off the ink. If it comes right off, any traces left on the fabrics will also wash right out of the quilt. Get a few dark colors, like red, green and black, so you'll have a color to contrast with everything. Don't buy

318.

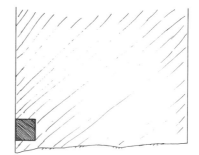

319.

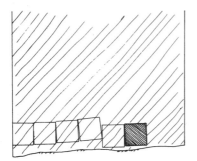

320.

a. Rhomboid   b. Trapezoid

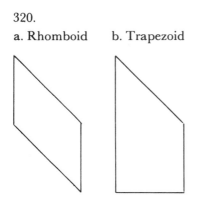

light grey or yellow hoping it will show up on dark fabrics; it won't. Only chalk or soap does that.

Lay out the pieces in rows across the fabric, as shown. If you have made the templates well, the pieces are supposed to fit neatly against each other. Of course they never do, but never mind. If the row of pieces begins to slant wildly up or down, break the row and start it back where it should be. It either means that you are drawing sloppily or that one of your angles is off by a hair. Just take care to use the point of the pen at an angle so the line will be as tight against the template as possible.

You always mark on the wrong side of the fabric, and with most shapes you can use the template with either side up. However, some irregular shapes, like the rhomboid in *Ribbons* or the trapezoid in *Road to Oklahoma,* have a definite right side and wrong side; the template can only be used one way to make the right shape on the right side of the fabric. It's like a child's mirror-writing, because the back of the template is the mirror image of the front. Regular letters, like O or T, and regular shapes, like squares, read the same in the mirror as they do to the eye. But irregular letters, like F and K, are reversed in the mirror, and irregular shapes are reversed if you trace them with the wrong side up. If your pattern contains such a shape be sure you are quite clear about which side to use. Remember that the back of the template is up when you mark the back or wrong side of the fabric, so that the shape will be right-side around on the right side of the fabric.

When you are marking white or very light fabric, use a sharp #2 pencil. This eliminates the possibility of traces of ink left on the seam margins showing through the top when the pieces are sewn together and the margins folded under. If you are having trouble making the pencil mark show up, don't just exert more and more pressure, because the drag of the pencil will make the fabric slip beneath the template and that will throw off your measurements. Instead use a nylon tip marker, but make the line very swiftly and lightly; this will leave the lightest possible ink mark. (In any case the ink will wash out, but some carefully tended quilts will not be washed for years.)

MARKING FOR HAND-SEWING

If you are planning to do piecework by hand, you will have made window templates to allow you to mark on the seam line as well as on the cutting line. The line outside can be marked with ink as above, but the seam line should be marked with lead or chalk pencil because an ink mark so close to the finished surface of the piece is bound to show through unless the fabric is absolutely opaque. If you find the template is sliding a good deal as you trace the inside line, tape sand paper to the bottom side of the template; this helps it to grip the fabric. If you want to, you can take a chance using a nylon tip washable ink marker on the seam line, making a very light swift stroke, but you must be prepared to wash the piece as soon as the quilting is finished.

To trace the seam line on dark fabric you can use a cake of tailor's chalk or a pencil; both are available at notions stores. I prefer pencil because it is easier to sharpen, but whichever you choose be prepared to sharpen often. Chalk goes dull very quickly and a dull marker makes a fat, inaccurate line.

CUTTING

Each piece of patchwork is cut out separately, using care and very sharp scissors. Fabric shears should never be used for anything except fabric because anything else (*especially* paper) dulls the blades. If you don't have a good pair, you might think of investing in one; you'll never appreciate sharp blades more than when you cut patchwork. Wiss, an American make, is the best brand and the one most readily available. The English and the Swiss are also known for good cutlery, though I can't guarantee any specific kinds; the Japanese brands are impressive-looking and usually cost about half the price of others, but they can't be sharpened, so every time they get dull you have to throw them away and buy a new pair. Good dressmaker's shears should have blades of forged steel; look for an announcement to that effect engraved on the blade, or ask the salesperson.

If you have a good pair of scissors but have been using them to trim hair or sever chicken wings, you can have them sharpened. Notions stores often offer that service and so do people who make or duplicate keys, for some reason. Keep your eyes open around your neighborhood for signs in locksmith's shops and hardware stores and you will probably find a scissors sharpener under your very nose.

A versatile pair of fabric scissors for most kinds of jobs should have blades about 4″, but you might also want a small pair, with blades about 1½″, for clipping threads and ripping seams. You can do these jobs with larger scissors if you are careful but if you are working quickly there is always a chance that you might snip a hole where you didn't want one with the tip of the blades.

When you have cut out all the pieces, sort them into piles according to shape and color. Some people like to run a thread through each pile to keep them separate. To do this, thread the needle but don't knot it; pass the thread from front to back and up again to front. Each piece can then be slipped off as you need it. However, I wouldn't bother with this unless you are moving the work around a great deal; for machine work especially, simple piles will be more convenient.

MARKING AND CUTTING NARROW STRIPS FOR LATTICE, BORDERS, OR BINDING

When you need long narrow strips of fabric for some phase of quiltmaking, you cannot easily make a template from which to trace them because posterboard doesn't come in large enough sheets.

Instead you can either tear the fabric into long even strips, or measure and draw parallel lines onto the fabric and cut the strips with scissors.

Tearing the fabric is the most desirable alternative because it saves you the rather annoying task of measuring and drawing, but it is only possible if the fabric has a firm straight weave, and tears in an absolutely straight line. Before you begin, work out on paper the total length of stripping you need, then decide whether it will be more economical for you to make strips across the fabric or down its length. This will depend upon the size of the quilt top, the length of the piece of fabric, and where you want the seams to fall if two strips must be sewn together to reach the length or breadth of the patchwork.

Next, test the fabric to see if it tears straight. If you are making strips across the fabric, make a short clip with scissors into the selvedge (side edge) of the fabric near one end of the piece. Take the fabric in two hands, one on either side of the cut, and with a strong firm yank, tear the fabric all the way across. If the raw width of the strip is to be 2¾″, measure that distance on the selvedge above the torn edge, clip the selvedge at the mark, and tear again. Measure the width of the resulting strip at four or five points; it should be exactly 2¾″ wide all the way across. If it is, you can make all the strips as you made this one. But if it varies by more than ¼″, you had better measure and draw the lines for cutting all the way across the fabric.

To draw parallel lines across the fabric, you must first manage one straight line all the way across exactly at right angles to the selvedge of the fabric. To do this, fold up a cuff of material on the end of the piece about an inch or so deep. Match the selvedge of the cuff to the selvedges of the piece and pin them. Smooth and flatten the resulting fold with your hand, pin it in place, and iron it flat. The resulting crease should be at right angles to both selvedges all the way across.

Next you must construct and draw a line

321. Cuff pinned in place

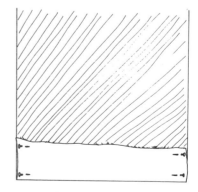

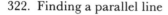

322. Finding a parallel line

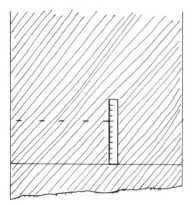

parallel to the crease. This is an easy matter if you have something with a straight edge longer than 45″ (or the width of the fabric). If you have a nice clean board or something that will serve, you can measure and mark the proper distance from the crease at each side of the fabric, lay the straight edge across the fabric connecting the two marks and draw the line. Otherwise, it is necessary to measure and mark a series of dots across the fabric in much the way that you measure and mark dots outside the seam line in order to add seam margins to a template.

Use a T-square as shown if you have one, or if you don't, use a ruler with the end squarely on the crease and the measuring edge perpendicular to it. Measure and mark each selvedge 2¾″ above the crease, then make a series of about five dots across the fabric, each exactly 2¾″ above the crease. You will then be able to connect the dots with a yardstick or other straight edge without fear of the line dipping or swaying in the middle. Continue until you have drawn all the strips you need, then cut along the lines with a sharp scissors.

MACHINE-PIECING

Begin by making one complete block to hang alongside your machine or carry in your work bag. This is partly for fun and partly to use as a guide so you can keep checking to make sure you are not sewing 200 squares to the wrong sides of 200 triangles. One color of thread is fine for the whole quilt top; I usually use off-white, but any light neutral color will do. The best thread is cotton-wrapped polyester, which only comes in one weight; it is stronger than pure cotton thread without being fat. (Fat thread makes big holes in the fabric, weakening it.) If you must use cotton thread, use mercerized #50. The machine needle should be size 14, the stitch length about 10 per inch. (Longer is too weak and shorter is too hard to rip out when you make a mistake.)

SEW THE SMALL UNITS
OF THE BLOCK FIRST

A block is built by joining all the smallest units, then the units of the next size, then joining them to each other in stages until the block is done. For example, if you were doing *Windmill,* you would join all the small squiggly triangles to all the small white ones (Fig. 324). You would then sew these to the matching large triangles, making four squares, then join the four four squares.

You don't need to baste the small units. Just match them carefully, right sides together, and run them through the machine, carefully guiding the margin edge against the appropriate mark on the throatplate. You don't need to backstitch or knot the thread to secure the stitching; each seam will be crossed by another seam, which will lock it.

BASTING OFF CENTER

When you are dealing with some shapes having long diagonal edges, there is a special trick to positioning them so that the edges will be even when you open out the seam after sewing. For example, if you sew two diamonds with the right sides together as shown (a), when you open them out they look like this (b).

To correct for this, you must position the two pieces off center by the width of the seam margin. If you have such a piece in your block, experiment with the position by placing pins along the line where the seam will go; open the work out, and adjust the pins until the edges match. Once you have one basted so that the edges match when the pieces are opened flat, use it as a model for positioning the others until all the blocks are made.

IRONING

When you have finished sewing the smallest units in the block, press them before sewing them to the next group. This is to insure that you don't sew in any folds or puckers when you sew across the first seam, which you might if it were not pressed

323. *Windmill*

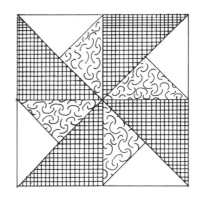

324.

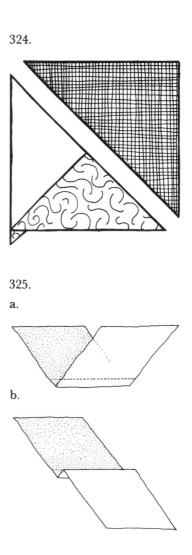

325.

a.

b.

flat. (Generally, it is best never to sew a second seam across a first until the first one has been pressed.)

Use steam if you have it, and if you are quite sure all your fabrics are pure cotton, use the cotton setting on the iron. If you think any of the fabrics are synthetics or blends, use the high end of the Permanent Press setting (right below Wool). Iron patchwork on the right side; don't try to press open the seam margins, as you do in dressmaking, for the margins are too narrow to handle without ironing off the ends of your fingers as well. (Open seams are a disadvantage during quilting anyway.)

Underneath the work, try to have the margins fall all on one side of the seam or the other; sometimes they try to cross in the middle. If possible, they should fall toward the darkest fabric, because they show through light ones. Use the tip of the hot iron in short, nudging strokes to force the top sides of the seam to open out crisp and flat.

BUILD THE SMALL UNITS INTO LARGER ONES

If you are making the *Windmill* block, first you join the smallest triangles (making a larger triangle) and press; sew these pieces to the matching triangle pieces (making squares) and press again. Then you join two squares, making rectangles, and again press. There is no need to baste these pieces before sewing.

Up to this point you can position the pieces for sewing by simply lining up the edges. But with larger units such as these two rectangles that both have seams down the center, the important thing is to make the seams meet *exactly*; matching the edges doesn't matter, because they will be underneath the finished work and no one will care. At this stage, it is necessary to pin baste the block at the joint where the center seams come together. Place the pieces right sides together; adjust them until the seams are precisely together and secure them with a pin right beside the joint, perpendicular to the line to

326.

a.

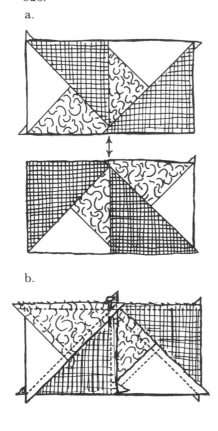

b.

be sewn. Don't remove this pin when you sew up to it; leave it till the seam is completed. This is standard practice. The sewing machine needle nearly always misses the pin or glances off it before or behind. One time in a thousand it lands squarely on the pin; this might bend or break the pin but it won't hurt the needle or sewing machine. Sew and press the seam, and the block is done.

ASSEMBLING THE REST OF THE BLOCKS

Once you have made the first block you can go on and finish the other blocks one at a time, which is very organic and satisfying, or if time is a factor (as it always is with me), make yourself an assembly line. Take all the pieces of the first size unit, such as the two smallest triangles in *Windmill*, and sew all you need for the entire quilt top. Press all the seams open, then sew all the first units to the second and so on, so that you complete all the blocks at the same time.

When you finish a seam during ordinary sewing, you usually clip the top and bobbin threads to free the work from the machine, then you pull out a length of top thread and of bobbin thread and hold them out behind the presser foot with one hand as you begin the next line of sewing. When you are working on patchwork, sewing one short seam after another, you can save a great deal of time and motion by not stopping to clip each piece free from the machine. Instead, as you finish a seam on one piece, pull the whole piece a few inches out behind the presser foot, taking the top and bobbin threads with it, and hold it there as you start the next seam on the next piece. When you've finished you'll have a monstrous chain of little pieces all connected and dangling a few inches apart. Clip the threads that join the pieces, and press the seams open as usual. Don't worry about pruning the dangling threads close to the material; they'll all be inside the quilt and won't matter.

JOINING THE BLOCKS TO FINISH

When all the blocks are sewn, join them first into horizontal rows the width of the quilt top, then sew each row to the next with one long seam until the entire top is finished. Here again, matching the edges of the work doesn't matter; the important

327.

a. Sewing blocks into a row

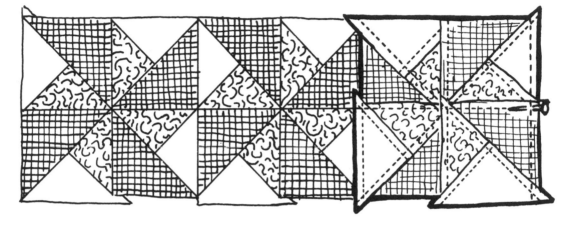

thing is to make each seam in the pattern meet precisely the corresponding seam in the adjoining pattern. As you position each block to the next, pin-baste each joint of the pattern very carefully, and when you sew the long seams to join the rows,

b. Rows basted at each joint

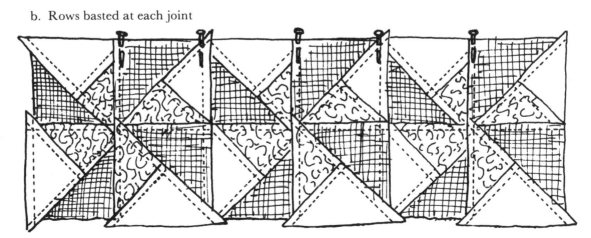

match and baste each joint within the block and the seams between the blocks as well. Stretch and ease the pieces as much as you have to to make the seams meet precisely. When one unit is much larger than the one it is supposed to match, you may even have to sew in some puckers, but with puffy batting behind it puckering isn't nearly as obvious as seams that don't meet would be.

There will be variations in the sizes of the pieces and hence in the precision with which they fit together; patchwork is a craft, not a science. The larger and more complex the units, the more cumulative the variations will be—this is unavoidable. If you've drafted your templates well and traced and cut carefully you shouldn't have much trouble. Up to a point, you can fudge, and the better you get at fudging the better you are at your craft.

By the time you get to the long seams, the edges will probably look like this. At this point, you

328.

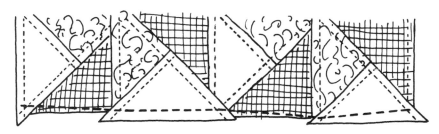

can take a few liberties with straightness of the seam. Try to cross each joint at the ⅜″ margin, but between the joints you can weave around a little. Be careful never to sew closer than ¼″ to the edge of a piece, even if it means taking a ½″ seam margin on the piece next to it. A pucker is better than a hole, and if you press the bejesus out of it, once the batting and quilting are added you'll hardly know the difference.

329.

a. Running stitches

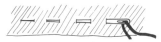

b. Backstitch for strength

330.

a.

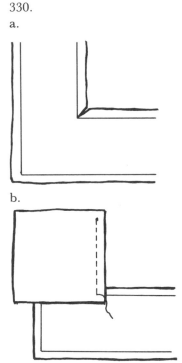

b.

331.

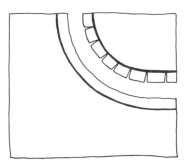

HAND-PIECING

For hand-piecing straight-seam blocks you follow the same order of construction as for machine. Use a needle size 8-10 sharp, cotton-wrapped polyester thread or, if you can get it, quilting thread. This is a strong cotton thread treated with silicone to prevent knotting; it is ideal for all hand-sewing as well as for quilting. There are at least three brands of quilting thread on the market, but it is very hard to get in urban areas. If you can't find it and your thread is tying itself in knots, take a shorter length of thread to start with, and if that doesn't help, get a lump of beeswax from the notions store and coat each length of thread before you start to sew. (That's what people did before they discovered silicone.)

Start each line of sewing with a knot or a backstitch, and proceed with the most even small running stitch you can, taking 3 or 4 stitches at a time, as shown. After every 3 or 4 stitches, add a backstitch for strength. End each seam with a backstitch, and press as described for machine-piecing, or if you don't have an iron handy take great care not to sew in any puckers.

SETTING IN ANGLES

To set a piece into an angle: carefully clip the margin to the corner, as shown. Sew one side of the figure almost to the corner. Stop and pin-baste the second side in place, taking great care to match and baste the seam line corners drawn on each piece. Turn the seam exactly at the corner and sew the second side.

CURVED SEAMS

To sew curved seams, carefully clip the convex curve almost to the margin about every ¾″ (331). Pin baste the pieces between each clip, starting in the center and working to each corner as smoothly as possible. Be careful not to strain or tear the fabric at the clip marks. Sew by hand (or machine), using very small stitches, and press with steam.

HAND-PIECING ONE-PATCHES

Patterns such as *Hexagons,* and *Baby's Blocks* are made with a different technique, one more typical of English than American patchwork. Using a window template or one without margins, trace the seam line of each piece in pencil or chalk on the wrong side of the fabric. If you are using a no-margin template, be sure to leave about ¾″ between each outline, and as evenly as you can cut about ⅜′ all the way around outside the seam line.

Next cut out a number of paper patterns exactly the size of the finished shape of the piece, without margins. The paper should be stiffer than, say, newsprint, but soft enough to be sewn through easily. People used to use pages from copy books, or they would cut up old letters for this, but for those of us who depend heavily on postcards and the telephone, construction paper, old Christmas cards, or the pages of a good sketch pad do nicely. If they are handled with care the papers may be used several times, so you only need to cut about half as many papers as fabric pieces.

Center a paper pattern exactly within the drawn seam line on the wrong side of the piece, and baste it with a pin. Fold in the fabric margin at the seam line on one side and thread-baste it in place through three layers of fabric and paper. At the corner, neatly fold the margins over the paper angle and catch them with the basting thread to make the angle sharp and accurate. Continue basting the next side and so on until all sides and corners are basted down. This assures that all angles will be as exact as necessary if the pieces are to fit together, and it eliminates the wad of seam margins you would otherwise have to sew through.

Naturally these extra steps take extra time. I recommend it, and I think it's worth it, because it ensures very good results. But if it sounds like horseradish to you, try one bunch with papers and one without and see which you like better. Some people manage just fine, especially on small projects, just sewing things together.

332. Using a no-margin template for marking and cutting

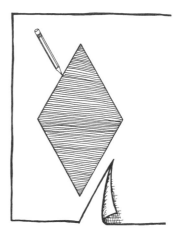

333. Basting down margins over paper pattern

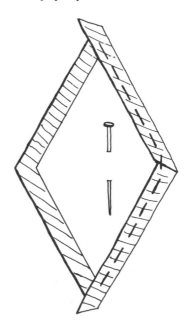

159

334. Assembly of 6-pointed star

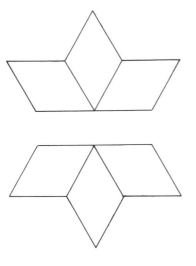

To assemble the pieces: when sewing a straight seam, hold the pieces, right sides together, and whip them with small stitches through the edges of the fold. Open out and set the next piece into the angle with a slipstitch, sewing back and forth from folded edge to folded edge. Take care to fit them tightly together; otherwise you may have holes at the corners. Assemble with a series of straight seams wherever possible for pleasant sewing and to avoid gaps at corners. For instance, patterns with stars (*Star and Blocks, Star and Hexagon*) should be assembled as shown.

When the piece has other pieces sewn to it on all sides, the paper can be removed and used again. Press the piece, then cut and pull out the basting thread, and the paper will drop out intact.

APPLIQUÉ BLOCKS

Appliqué patches are traced from templates having no seam margins; the line you draw is the sewing line, so trace with pencil or chalk. The back or wrong side of the template is the reverse—mirror image—of the front; you trace on the wrong side of the fabric with the wrong side of the template up, so that the shape will be the right way around when you turn the piece right side up. As you trace, space the outlines at least ¾″ apart. Cut out each piece with sharp scissors ¼″ to ⅜″ outside the drawn line, to make a margin for turning under.

To prepare the work for sewing: on each shape to be appliquéd, clip the seam margins at convex curves and at all corners to allow the margins to fold smoothly under the finished shape. Center the posterboard template within the drawn lines on the wrong side of the piece; a little at a time, fold the margins to the inside over the posterboard and press with a hot iron to make a sharp crease.

Take the background square to which the shapes will be appliquéd, fold it in quarters, and press briefly. The resulting lines will cross exactly in the center and provide a guide with which to position the shapes, so that each block will be the

335. Clip at curves and corners

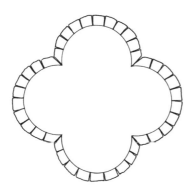

same. (If the pattern is diagonal, fold the block corner to corner and press.) Pin-baste the pieces to the square, adjusting until they look the way you want them to. Not all edges must be hemmed; wherever possible the raw edge of one piece will be tucked under the hemmed edge of the next. For example, in *Tulip* the edges of the petals are tucked under the center oval and the base of the leaves are tucked under the stem. If you want a raised effect in any portion of the design, tuck a tuft of quilt batting under the piece before you baste it down.

When all pieces are basted in place, sew them down with a small, invisible hemming stitch. Take a stitch through the fold of the appliqué shape, then pick up a thread or two of the background material. The thread should match the appliqué pieces. If you prefer, you can use a decorative top-stitch, like a blanket stitch, and in that case you may prefer to use contrasting thread colors.

To do an overall appliqué pattern like this baby quilt (Fig. 337), first draw the entire design on graph paper, then determine the scale of the finished piece as you would for piecework. (In other words, each graph paper square stands for 2″, or whatever you like.) Measure and piece the background areas in appropriate sizes and colors, and if necessary measure and press in guide lines to help you position the small appliqué pieces. For example, you might want to fold and press in a crease from top to bottom along the right side of the house to help locate the tulips and the bottom of the path and the dog. Objects that stand free in the pattern, like the tulips or the gingham dog, cn be drawn freehand to scale on graph paper or any paper, and the drawing can be used as a template to trace and cut pieces of fabric. For elements like the tree trunk, the smoke, or the path, which must fit exactly, you may want to place tracing paper directly over the area and draw the figure exactly where and how you want it to look. Cut out the drawing from the tracing paper and use it as a template to mark and cut the fabric

336. *Tulip* (1)

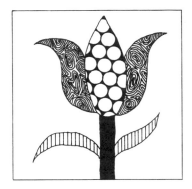

336a.

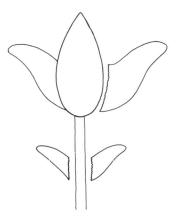

piece. Remember, the wrong side of the drawing is up when you mark the wrong side of the fabric. The seam margins are clipped and pressed in, and the figures basted in place and hemmed down.

If you don't use such a structured background, you can dispense with the drawn plan altogether. Just cut a background of one or two pieces, say, white and blue for land and sky. Then, keeping some consistent scale in mind, draw and cut out whatever you feel like putting in the picture—sun, clouds, trees, flowers, animals, people—and move them around the quilt top like pins in a strategy map until you find an arrangement that pleases you. Then baste and hem them in place.

MACHINE APPLIQUÉ

If you don't mind having your stitches show, there's no reason why you shouldn't appliqué with a machine top-stitch. As always, this is much faster than hand-sewing, but not necessarily easier; keep in mind that every little goof or skip or snag shows for all the world to see if you're top-stitching.

If you'd like to try it, prepare the appliqué pieces exactly as for hand-sewing, with margins pressed under and everything. Baste firmly, and make sure the bobbin on the machine is full, because you'll hate yourself if you run out halfway around a piece. The line of stitching must be locked at beginning and end (and in the middle if you run out of bobbin.) To lock the stitching, you can use a few backstitches, which show, or you can leave enough top thread at each end to thread through a needle, draw to the underside of the fabric and tie in a knot with the bobbin thread.

Sew around each piece with small straight stitches, staying as close to the edge as you can, or use a short, decorative zig-zag stitch. Try a test piece before you approach the quilt to see which you prefer. I believe the straight stitch is harder to handle because every little waver in the line shows glaringly and embarrasses you.

339.
a. Straight stitch

b. Zig-Zag

c. Satin stitch

If your machine does satin-stitching, you can use it to appliqué in matching or contrasting colors of thread. In this case the wide, glossy lines of stitching form a pattern in their own right, and you need not bother to hem the edges of the appliqué piece because the thread encloses all raw edges and prevents raveling. Use the widest zig-zag setting, and keep the whole width of the stitch just inside the edge of the appliqué shape. If any raw edges extend beyond the stitching, shave them off with sharp scissors, being careful not to cut the thread or the fabric beneath.

REVERSE APPLIQUÉ

In reverse appliqué the pattern is cut out of a piece (rather than sewn onto it), then the piece is mounted on another of contrasting color which shows through the cut-out. It is a difficult technique, not used much in quiltmaking, although it is perfectly suited to it if you're able.

Like regular appliqué the design can be anything from patchwork geometrics to pictures of ducks, but a large regular shape will be *much* easier than a small involved one. Fig. 340 shows a possible block pattern for a reverse appliqué quilt. To make a template in this design or one of your own, draw the block to scale on graph paper, transfer the block to posterboard, and then with sharp scissors or a matte knife cut out and discard all the pattern pieces (shown in black in the illustration) leaving the rest of the block intact. Add seam margins around the outside of the block and cut.

With this template, outline the block and holes in pencil or chalk on the top fabric (here conceived as white). With sharp scissors cut out the center of the pattern holes, leaving about ¼″ seam margin all around the inside of the seam line. Carefully clip the margins to the seam line at each angle. Press the margins to the wrong side.

Center the white pattern block over a dark square of the same size and baste, especially

340. Reverse appliqué block

341. Pattern traced on foreground fabric, with margins clipped

around the holes. With invisible hemming stitches or tiny blanket stitches, sew the pattern piece to the background around the holes. Baste around the edges of the block to prevent the layers from shifting, and assemble the blocks as for any quilt. Keep in mind that the background of each block could be a different fabric, or that you can piece the background so that one color shows through half the holes and another through the other half.

CRAZY QUILTS

Instead of sewing all the crazy pieces to each other in an endless sheet, as colonial women did, crazy quilts these days are built on foundation pieces of fabric, usually blocks, and organized and assembled just like sane quilts.

Start by cutting squares of muslin of the number and size you need for the finished top. (Fifteen inches square is a good size.) Cut a piece of top fabric with two sides at right angles and thread-baste it to the corner of the square, as shown. Press or fold a hem down on one side of the next piece and baste it in place over the raw edge of the first. Be careful to overlap enough so that the raw edge won't slip out. Continue in this manner until the entire block is filled, always covering raw edges with folded ones.

You can then finish the sewing with invisible hem stitches, but a more usual approach is to use decorative embroidery stitches in threads of contrasting colors along all the seams. If you don't know how to embroider, you can find little booklets of embroidery stitches at notions stores and fabric departments; such glossaries are also given in women's and sewing magazines from time to time.

A more contemporary approach is used in Fig. 344, *Pace Victoria.* Here each piece was stuffed with a little quilt batting to give a riased, puffy effect before the next piece was basted over it. The finish sewing is done in a variety of machine embroidery

342. Corner piece basted to foundation block

343. Hemmed edge of second piece basted over raw edge of first

344. *Pace Victoria*, 39″ × 50″. Author's crazy quilt.

stitches by my magic Singer (though a simple satin stitch would do as well.) The outline of the overall patterns was pencilled on a piece of muslin, the crazy part filled in, and the columns and corners were appliquéd on last over all the raw edges. This technique could be used for any other combination of crazy quilting and appliqué. Why, you could make an appliqué picture of a madhouse, with crazy quilting in all the windows.

This particular quilt has no batting other than stuffed patches, and no lining either, since the pattern on the back made by the embroidery stitches is almost as interesting as the front. If you embroider well or know a machine that does, you could easily decorate an entire quilt top with stitches alone. I discovered on this project that a special interest is added to the reverse side of the machine satin stitching if the bobbin thread is a different color from the top thread.

BORDERS

Decorative borders can be pieced or appliquéd using the techniques described for making the top itself. The piecework is composed in long strips, the appliqué is sewn to a long strip of background material cut or torn to the proper dimensions and pressed down the middle to provide a guiding crease against which to center the design. Plain borders are cut and pieced using the same technique as for making a lattice stripping.

The width of the border will depend partly on what the pattern needs esthetically to set it off, partly on what is required to fill out the dimensions of the finished quilt. A solid border 5″ to 8″ wide is usually an effective frame, as is a narrow white border within a dark one, as in Fig. 47, *Clay's Choice* (page 66).

Before you decide whether to cut strips for a border across the fabric or lengthwise, be sure to think carefully about where, or whether, you want seams. If you must have seams, plan to center them. All borders are cut to the finished dimen-

345. Straight corners

sions plus ⅜″ margins on all sides, unless the border is also to be the binding (see Finishing).

There are several ways to apply a border. A narrow border, plain or pieced, frames the quilt on four sides. The easiest plan is to put on borders the exact length of the top (including margins), then add borders across the width of the top, as shown. Mitered corners are a little more trouble, but they are handsome if done well. To miter: let the lengthwise strips extend beyond the corners by at least the width of the border (a). Sew the end borders across the quilt top *only*, having the ends extend by the same amount (b). Open out the end border and fold the extensions under, forming a 45° angle, as shown (c). Hand-stitch the diagonal fold in place, and repeat for each corner.

a.

b.

c.

346. Mitering a corner

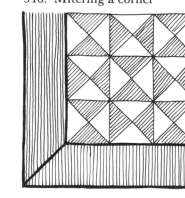

Decorative borders may be planned and applied the same way, but corners are usually more of a problem if the border is pieced or appliquéd, for whether you use squared strips or miters it is rather tricky to make the pattern meet exactly at the seam. It may be that your quilt top fits together beautifully and according to your calculation is exactly 80″ wide. But when you piece together a nifty strip of checkerboards and try to baste it to the top, you find that the top is really 78 ¾″ and the checkerboards in the corners are having nothing to do with each other. It is very difficult to adjust for such small variation in a large measurement, especially since few of us have adequate work space to do perfect measuring and cutting on that scale. Traditional quiltmakers often got around this problem by putting a blank square in the corners of the border, or one with a contrasting pattern. This doesn't alter the fact that the dimensions are off, but it makes it far less glaring. If the border is wide enough, the square could even be a block from the pattern of the top.

FINISHING

For reasons you will understand after you read the quilting chapter (if you don't already), you can't sew up the sides of a quilt before you stuff it, as you would a pillow. The edges are finished last, usually by hand. (The only exception to this is a baby quilt with a dacron batting. If you are very careful not to put your hand through the batting or snag it during handling, you can sew up three sides, turn the piece right side out, and slip stitch the last side.)

Very often traditional quilts were finished with a narrow binding, like blanket binding, in a color contrasting with the top and/or border. This was partly for esthetics, and partly because the edges of the quilt tended to get shredded from being stretched very tightly on the frame and they had to be completely enclosed to prevent raveling.

This binding might serve as a border, or as an addition to it.

Binding can be cut with the weave, like lattice strips, or on the bias, although bias binding is only really important for curved or irregular edges, because it stretches. Use it for binding scallops, or for a jagged edge like the one on the *Grand Army* quilt. To find true bias, fold one selvedge across the fabric till the lengthwise threads parallel the cross-wise threads, and press. Measure and cut strips parallel to the crease about 2″ wide and piece them to the required length.

For straight binding, cut strips 2″ to 5″ wide. The quilt to which binding is applied should have edges of the top, the batting, and backing all even. The binding is pin-basted to the quilt top, right sides together, and sewn by hand or machine through all the layers: binding, top, batting, and backing. This secures the edge of the batting all around, an advantage if the quilting pattern does not extend clear to the edges of the piece. Sew the long sides first, then the ends, mitering corners or not, as described above. Turn under the free edge of the binding ¼″ to ½″ to form a hem, and pin-baste to the back of the quilt, taking care to cover the line of machine-stitching. Hand-stitch in place with invisible hemming stitches.

An alternative plan is to use the edge of the backing to bind. To do this you cut the backing 1½″ wider than the top on all sides. After quilting, turn forward a small hem on the edge of the backing and baste it to the front of the quilt all around. Hem in place. Like binding, this finishes the quilt with a narrow strip of contrasting color.

If you prefer no contrasting strip to show, you can use the edge of the border to bind to the back. Measure the border an extra 1½″ wide to account for turning and hemming. (You can trim the back and batting after quilting to accomplish this if necessary.) Turn under a hem on the border, baste to the back, and hem in place. Try to pick up a

349.

little batting with each stitch, to secure its edges on all sides, but be sure not to have your stitches show through to the front. Also with any of these finishing methods you are free to machine-stitch instead of blind hemming. Only keep in mind, if you do, that top-stitching is very obvious and ought to be done well. (One of the great points in favor of hemming by hand is that, since it is invisible, no one can tell how well or badly it was done. As long as the quilt doesn't fall apart, you're home free.) Always start top-stitching with a full bobbin and try to keep the stitching straight and parallel to the edge.

If you prefer another method, you can cut both top and backing the same size and trim the batting 1' or so smaller around. Turn the edges of the top and back inside and baste and hem them together. Use this technique if for some reason you want no border or frame at all to show around the edge of the quilt. It is also suitable for top-stitching. Its only disadvantage is that it does not secure the batting at all—again, a consideration especially if you have used a spare quilting pattern.

ADDING A WIDE SKIRT TO THE QUILT

The last method of finishing is to add an unstuffed wide border or skirt to the quilted top like the one on the *Hayes' Corner* quilt, Fig. 55 (page 71). This is by far the most disagreeable method of finishing because it demands accurate measuring, cutting, and basting on an enormous scale, and in general it seems that the larger a piece of work is, the more can go wrong.

The pieced top of *Hayes' Corner* is 80" × 100"—the size of the top of the client's bed, plus extra length to cover pillows. Since the owner wanted to use it as a daytime bedspread, it needed a wide border to cover the box spring and so on, but there was no possibility of simply adding a border to the top before quilting because the largest batting made is only 90" x 108"—not large enough.

(Piecing batting is not a good idea unless you are going to quilt much more closely than most modern quilters care to.)

I decided to finish the quilt top and then add a border 22″ wide as if it were an enormous binding. I had then to measure, cut, and piece borders for the sides and end, plus ⅜″ seam margins on all sides. (The top edge needed only a binding, since the head of the bed is against the wall.) Measuring such pieces is very difficult without a cutting table 100″ long, or a very large clean floor space that no dogs or babies are going to walk across the minute you lay out the fabric. Lacking that, you must measure with a yardstick as best you can, but since the measurements can't possibly be exactly right, be sure they are a little too long, rather than a little too short.

If the border is to reach to the floor, the corners must be rounded off to prevent their dragging halfway across the room. To do this, cut the corner square the proper size, with seam margins. Make an ersatz compass by tying a long string around a pencil. Place the pencil point exactly in the corner of one seam line and with a pin or your thumb hold the taut string firmly on the seam line at the adjacent corner. Draw an arc from the pencil's corner to the corner opposite. Be sure to hold the pencil perpendicular to the line as you draw; tilting it will change the length of the string and you will not get a perfect arc. If the arc is perfect, it will hit the second corner exactly.

Cut out the resulting shape, leaving a seam margin outside the arc, and use it as a template to cut three more.

Because the corners must be handled in this way, the entire border must be constructed in duplicate, a top and a facing. You need four border pieces and four equal pieces of plain backing material. The facing pieces are cut to the same dimensions as the top pieces, plus 1½″ on all inside edges for hemming.

350.

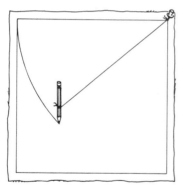

351. Top

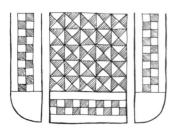

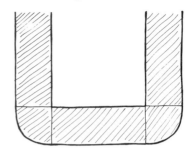

Sew the border pieces to the quilt top as shown (351), end piece first, then sides. Stich through all layers to secure batting; if the end piece is too long, I think it is better to center it and cut a little off each end than to create an imbalance by having it perfect at one side and off at the other. If the side pieces are too long, place them correctly at the foot, and cut off extra at the head where it will hardly show. If any of them are too short, have a cup of warm milk and go to bed; tomorrow you can decide where to add on a piece, or whether to start over.

When the border is on and pressed, sew together the facing as shown. Baste it right sides together to the border, and sew all the way around. Clip seam margins carefully at the curves; turn, and press. Turn under a hem and baste to the inside of the quilt top, taking all possible care to see that the skirt hangs smoothly. This is by far the hardest part, for some reason. If by chance you have enough floor space, the best choice would be to lay the entire quilt out flat to baste. If not, the second-best plan is to place the quilt on the bed it was made for and baste as it hangs, so you can see if it begins to pull and pucker. If neither of these is possible, drape the quilt over a table, having the top of the border at the edge and one corner at a corner of the table. Baste as far as you can in two directions, working from the corner, then shift the quilt so you can baste the other sides the same way. When you are sure that the skirt hangs smoothly all around, hem or top-stitch the facing in place. Bind the head end with a strip of appropriate material.

9 QUILTING

Tools: Pencil, Chalk, Yardstick, Batting (available in some department stores or by mail order—see list of sources at the back of the book.)

NOT QUILTING

Before I become specific about designs and techniques for quilting, perhaps I ought to face the possibility that you may not want to quilt; some people don't, I'm told. If this is the case, yet you want to make a coverlet that is as warm as a quilt, the easiest solution is to make the top and back it with that prequilted material they sell for making bathrobes. It is available in any fabric store and some of it is actually rather nice.

To use prequilted material for backing, cut and piece a sheet of it the same size as the quilt top. Baste the backing to the quilt top right sides together, and machine-stitch around three sides of the work. Cut across the seam margins diagonally at the corners, and turn the work right side out, being sure to poke out the corners until they look square. Turn in the remaining free edges of the top and backing to inside, and slip stitch them together. Then with the quilt spread smooth, place a few hidden tacks here and there (about one per three square feet) to prevent the layers from shifting.

TACKING

To tack, thread a needle with a color of thread that won't show on the top. Tie a tight, small knot at the end of the thread, and bring the needle up through the quilt from back to front. Pull gently until you feel the knot pop through the backing into the batting (don't pull it all the way out the front). Take two or three tiny backstitches, one on top of the other, through all layers, then run the needle off into the batting and out the top again. Clip the thread end.

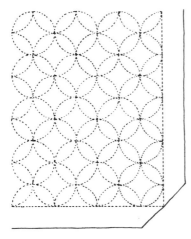

353. Clip margins at corners

354. Making a tack

174

USING A BLANKET AS A FILLER

Another way to avoid quilting is to use an old blanket as the filling layer of the spread. Be sure the blanket is completely preshrunk; if you're not sure, wash it and dry it a few times. Cut the blanket the same size as the backing and baste it smoothly to the wrong side (inside) of the backing. Pin-basting will do.

If you have to cut and piece the blanket to make it the right size, lay the pieces side by side with their edges overlapping 1″, and machine-stitch through the double thickness. This will be strong and will make a less lumpy seam than if you stitched right sides together. Baste the back-and-blanket piece to the top, right sides together, and sew three sides. Remove the basting pins and finish as above.

TYING

You can secure the layers of a quilt or comforter with decorative knots, tufts, or bows; this differs from tacking in that it is meant to show, and the knots are usually arranged in some rudimentary pattern. Knots are often used when the quilt is stuffed with something that can't be quilted. In hard times, war time, even into this century, people lined quilts with newspaper; quilts made to be given to the poor were very often made that way. In colonial days makers were reduced to stuffing quilts with leaves or corn cobs, and you can do this, too, if you don't know what to do with your old corn cobs.

In her *Quilting Manual*, D. A. Hinson reports that tie quilts or comforters, were sometimes made at quilting parties with the quilt stretched on a frame and the ladies seated around it, while the children played underneath where they could return the needle to the top after it was pushed down through the filler. The children claimed to enjoy helping and listening to the quilting party chatter, except that they never got to hear the end of the stories because the ladies always whispered when they got to the good parts.

355. Stitching through lapped edges

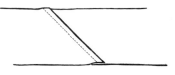

356.

a. Knot points on a grid

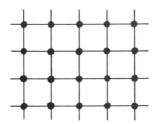

b. Knots in a pattern

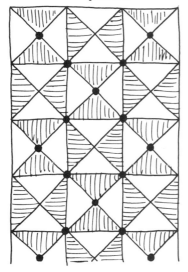

A tie comforter is still easy to make, either with several layers of dacron quilt batting or with a comforter bat from Sears Roebuck. Assembly is as follows: cut or piece a fabric backing the same size as the quilt top, and cut the batting an inch or two smaller. With a yardstick and pencil or chalk, mark the top on the right side into a grid for knotting, with the spaces not more than 7″ apart, or use a decorative pattern determined by the patchwork design, always taking care not to leave spaces larger than 7″ square.

If you like, you can mark the top into a grid by pressing in creases. Fold the top in half lengthwise; fold in half again and again until the long folded top is only 7″ wide, or less, then press the folded edges with a hot steam iron. When you unfold it, the piece will have a crease every 7″ from top to bottom. Fold the top in half across again and again until it measures about 7″ across, then press the folded edges again. When you unfold it, the piece will be creased in a 7″ grid.

Pin-baste the top and back together at one long edge, right sides together, and sew. Press open the seam. Spread the two pieces out on a table or the floor, wrong side up. Lay the batting on the backing and smooth out any wrinkles; lay the top on over both, as if you were closing the cover of a book.

KNOTS

Make knots at each point marked on the top of the comforter, using a needle threaded with washable acrylic yarn, buttonhole twist, crochet thread, or any strong decorative thread. Pass the needle through the comforter from front to back through all layers and up again very close to the point of entry. Be sure to leave a tail of thread on top with which to tie. Take another stitch in the same place in the same way for strength, ending again on top. Tie the two ends tightly in a bow or square knot or any other fancy knot you may know.

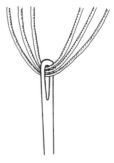

TUFTS

To make a tuft, make a knot as above, but use a needle with a large eye such as an embroidery or yarn darning needle, and thread it double with three or four strands of lightweight acrylic yarn. When you have finished you will have four or six strands of yarn trailing from the knot instead of two; clip the yarn close to the knot, and you have a handsome little clump.

BUTTONS

If you don't want knots *or* tufts, you can secure the quilt by sewing on decorative buttons through all layers. Sew them tightly as you would any button, except that you don't make a shank, since there is no need to accommodate a buttonhole.

SENDING THE TOP OUT FOR FINISHING

If you like, you can send the piece out to be commercially quilted (by machine). In the yellow pages of many large city directories, you can also find places that will stuff the quilt with down and tuft or quilt it. If you can't find such a place in your area, look for advertisements for commercial quilting in sewing and women's magazines, or write to Schacter's (see the list of mail order sources in the back of the book).

There is rumored to be an underground network of human quilters who mark and quilt the top for you by hand. I've had a little trouble locating these phantoms, but if you live in a rural area you can try calling church guilds or Ladies' Aid groups to see if it's still going on. That failing, write to the quilting department of the Stearns & Foster Company (see back for the address) and they will try to put you in touch with a quilter in your area.

CHOOSING BATTING AND PATTERNS

Welsh and English quilters still use wool for winter quilts, and cotton flannel is sometimes used to line a silk or velvet quilt, but cotton has been the American quiltmaker's staple from the late 18th century until the present day. It is light but warm, odorless, washable, and easy to sew through. However, since cotton occurs in nature in bolls, not sheets, the bat must be closely quilted over its entire surface or it will shred and shift and lump during washing and heavy use. This property of the cotton bat had a great deal to do with the evolution of popular quilting designs. If you are familiar with antique quilts you are aware that they often included four or five elaborate stitching patterns, such as grids and diamonds over pieced areas, eagles, whorls, roses, or pineapples in the plain areas, and rows and rows of feathers, loops, and scrolls along the borders. For more than a century quiltmakers took increasing pride in evolving ever more difficult and time-consuming designs with which to prevent the cotton from returning itself to bolls, until the trend inevitably passed the point of no return. By 1890 machine-made comforters could be bought in stores, improved heating methods made quilts less essential anyway, and people discovered they had better, or at least other things to do than quilt, such as demonstrating for women's suffrage or talking on the new telephone. (Susan B. Anthony made her first speech at a quilting bee, and that in itself went a good way toward stopping the quilting parties for a while.)

Not until the invention of the dacron bat did it become really feasible for 20th-century needlepeople to quilt their own quilts again. Dacron has all the advantages of cotton, but requires far less quilting because it is man-made in sheets, and used properly it holds together by itself; it doesn't have to be anchored down every inch to prevent lumping and tearing in the wash and in heavy use. Cotton is slightly less expensive than dacron, and it is not so springy, so that it tends to have a more satisfying heft to it. Nevertheless, I strongly urge you to use dacron, for the difference in price is really a false economy when you consider how vastly more time consuming it is to quilt cotton adequately. Even for those to whom time is not a consideration the dacron bat allows much more freedom of design.

If you prefer traditional cotton batting and have the skill and patience for it, you may also want to choose a traditional pattern to go with it. Ladies in the old days had a collection of quilting templates and perforated patterns they traded around. Nowadays, the best approach is to send for a catalogue of traditional perforated patterns from the Stearns and Foster Co. There is no point in attempting a traditional pattern if you don't mean to do it well, and the only way you can do that is by using a full-size, perfectly drawn pattern. Stearns and Foster has a handsome, well-made assortment, and they include instructions for marking the design onto the quilt top.

DESIGNING A QUILTING PATTERN

If you are using a dacron bat and plan to design your own pattern, you begin, again, by familiarizing yourself with what has been done before. You will find here patterns and instructions for all the various techniques that have been used in the past, but the way you choose to use and combine them will reflect nobody's taste but your own. Just keep in mind the prime difference between traditional and modern quilting design: the traditional design was a massive pattern, complete in itself, and imposed fairly irrelevantly over every inch of the quilt top, while the modern design is planned specifically to enhance and complement the patchwork pattern over which it is laid. A traditional quilt, well and beautifully quilted, generally makes you think, "What handsome patchwork! What noble quilting!" in two separate clauses, while a well-integrated modern design makes you think, "What a beautiful quilt!" without your being able to separate the two patterns in your mind.

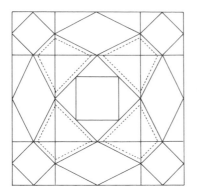

358. Quilting trapezoids in *Storm at Sea*

OUTLINE QUILTING

Perhaps the simplest traditional style of quilting is outline quilting; it is generally used on a busy or dramatic quilt top, where you want to be sure that the quilting doesn't compete or interfere with the patchwork. With a cotton bat, one was more or less obliged to outline every piece of patchwork; it took forever, but it was effective, especially if the patchwork was well designed in the first place. With a dacron bat you can be more selective about which pieces of patchwork to outline. The portions within the lines of quilting will puff up a little, especially after washing, so if you choose carefully which areas to emphasize, you can really add another dimension to the patchwork, make the pattern say something it wasn't saying before.

My own choice is to select either the most unusual or the least obvious area of the patchwork and outline it to throw it into relief. Thus in *Storm at Sea* I would outline the trapezoid (see the drawing), which is the least obvious geometric in this otherwise assertive pattern. In the *Wheels* quilt (page 113), I have outlined all the white areas to emphasize the peculiar shapes in the background of the pattern.

If your eye is very good, you can quilt lines parallel to the seams of the pieces to be outlined without marking the top at all. My eye is not, so I generally draw quilting lines on the quilt top in light pencil, using a dressmaker's T-square to keep them parallel to the seams. If you stitch very close to the seam lines this won't be necessary, but remember that if you stitch close to the seam lines you have to stitch through all the seam margins, which is much more difficult than simply quilting through top, lining, and batting. I think it is worth it to construct and draw parallel lines at least ⅜″ from the seam lines whenever possible.

On page 120, *Night and Day* shows a slightly more complicated pattern based on outline quilting. First outlines were drawn within the star

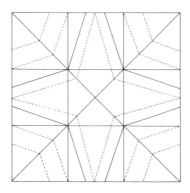

359. Quilted block from *Night and Day*

360. Diagonals

361. Squares

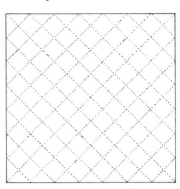

362. Corners

363. Diamonds

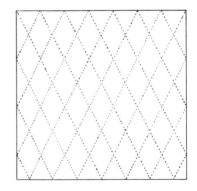

364. Boxes

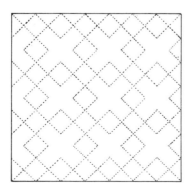

365. Lightning

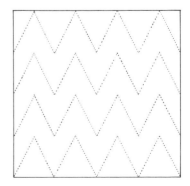

shapes, and then octagon shapes were drawn by making lines parallel to the outline of the star. It may sound like a lot of finicky measuring, but actually the whole pattern was drawn by eye with a pencil and the straight edge of a triangle. Unlike the process for making patchwork, in quilting if the pattern *looks right,* it *is* right.

OVERALL PATTERNS

Simple, overall quilting patterns are shown in the drawings and in Figs. 47 and 285 *(Clay's Choice* and *Red and White).* These are spaced according to the joints of the patchwork and can be drawn on the quilt top with a yardstick and a light pencil line, or chalk pencil or soap cut to a sharp edge for dark fabric. The stitching falls directly on the line so that the pencil shows a little or not at all after quilting, but be careful not to make it too dark and don't use a softer pencil than #2 (#1 will smudge).

If the pattern is made entirely of straight lines, it can be most quickly marked with a long string rubbed with colored chalk and a little help from a friend. Have the powdered string held taut across the entire quilt on the line you want marked, and snap it. If parts of the line fail to show on lighter fabrics, fill them in with pencil and a yardstick.

PERFORATED PATTERNS

If you prefer, you can make your own perforated pattern, either imitating traditional ones or depicting anything you like—your astrological sign, your initials, a picture or photograph. Draw or trace the design on tracing paper. Then perforate the pattern by running the quilting lines slowly and carefully under the unthreaded needle of the sewing machine, turning the wheel of the machine by hand.

To mark the design on the quilt, prepare two saucers of cornstarch, one white for dark fabrics, one darkened with cinnamon or powdered chalk.

366. *Chinese Puzzle*, 82″ × 102″. Author's quilt.

367. *Crazy Ann* detail

368. *Road to Oz* detail

Place the pattern over the quilt top in the area to be marked, then apply the powder to the perforations with a ball of cotton or quilt batting. Dab first to cover the holes with powder, then rub gently to be sure it penetrates evenly. Remove the paper and blow to scatter excess powder. This makes a neat, clear line of dots for you to follow. If they begin to smudge during quilting, reinforce the line with a light pencil before it disappears.

This sort of quilting will obviously be most effective in areas with little or no piecing; it is especially applicable to quilts set together with alternate pieced and plain blocks, where it need not compete with the patchwork design for attention.

PATTERNS MADE WITH STRING AND PENCIL COMPASS

It is also possible to make an overall pattern using circles or arcs as in Fig. 366, *Chinese Puzzle.* Use a pencil with a long string tied to it. If you have to reach halfway across a large quilt, as here, it will help a great deal if someone else holds the string at the center of the arc for you. Be sure to hold the pencil perpendicular to the line at all times so as not to change the length of the string, and go over the dark areas with chalk pencil before you lengthen the string for the next arc.

Figs. 367 and 368 show circles used in smaller repetitive designs to form the overall quilt pattern. *Crazy Ann* uses a large one and a small one, both drawn with string and pencil using the joints of the patterns to determine size.

TEACUP QUILTING

The Road to Oz (Fig. 368) has three concentric circles in each block centered by eye and drawn by the old teacup method. Teacup quilting was so named because you created a pattern by tracing around household objects like teacups; here, I believe, the objects were a glass, a saucer, and the lid of the baby's diaper pail.

369.

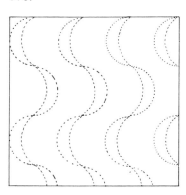

370.

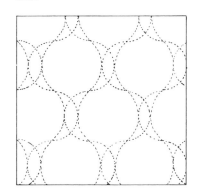

371.

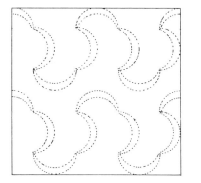

372.

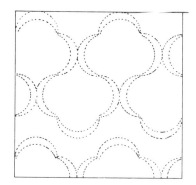

373.

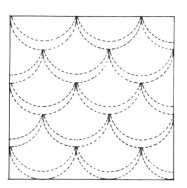

374.

375.
a. Trace around teacup

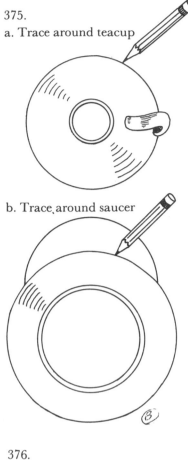

b. Trace around saucer

TEMPLATES FOR QUILTING PATTERNS

It is also possible to make patterns from templates. Here are a variety of patterns that can be made with a single crescent template.

To make a crescent, you need two circular objects, one larger than the other. On posterboard draw the outside edge of the crescent by tracing halfway around the smaller circle. Position the larger one as shown so that it forms a crescent of the desired size, and draw the inside curve of the template.

If you want to make a chain of squares, circles or ovals, make a posterboard template of the appropriate size and shape. Make one tracing of the shape on paper, then shift the template to where the next link should be. Notch the template where it intersects the traced lines; the notches will guide you so that all the links will be evenly spaced.

To draw an oval: cut a string about 15″ long. (You will have to experiment to achieve the right size for your pattern.) Lap the ends and splice with Scotch Tape, forming a smooth loop of string. Stick two thumb tacks or push pins into posterboard about 5″ apart, and place the loop over them (a). Holding a sharp pencil perpendicular to the posterboard, draw a continuous line all around the inside of the taut loop of string (b). The result should be a perfect oval. If necessary, change the size of the loop and distance between the push pins to get the size and shape oval you want.

376.
a. Notched template for chain of squares

b. For chain of circles

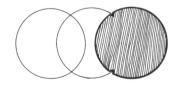

c. For chain of ovals

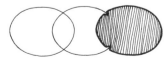

377.
a.

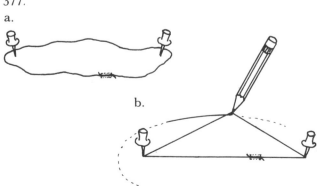

b.

RANDOM QUILTING

Quilting on dacron batting need not follow a regular pattern. You could make a totally random pattern freehand, or employ a template in a random way to soften a harsh or angular patchwork pattern. If you have made an abstract or pictorial appliqué quilt, you might try lines of quilting that roughly parallel the outlines of the figures, echoing outward until they lock with each other.

TESTING THE DESIGN

You can, of course, use a combination of these techniques for designing a quilt pattern. If you want to test the pattern or combination before you mark it onto the top, cover all or part of the patchwork with tracing paper. You can get large rolls of tracing paper from artists' or architects' supply stores. Very lightly, draw the pattern on the tracing paper with a *blunt* tip felt marker (such as a Magic Marker). This is better than pencil because you can make a dark line without using pressure, but be careful not to puncture the paper and stain the quilt. (Use a washable marker to be safe.) You will then be able to see the quilting pattern superimposed on the patchwork, and if you don't like it you can throw it away and try something else.

HOW MUCH QUILTING DO YOU NEED?

If you are using a cotton bat, you must have a line of stitching every two or three inches. If you use dacron you can leave much larger areas unquilted and the bat will still hold together in the wash, but don't misunderstand me; it will not look exactly as if you *had* quilted every two inches. It will get a little puffy and funky-looking, like a comforter. Any kind of batting puffs up around and between lines of stitches, so if you want it to puff up in exactly the way traditional cotton quilts did, you have to have as many lines of stitching as they did.

Unless the piece is to be a very formal bedspread, most people positively like the puffy

378.
a. Random lines

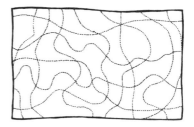

b. Hearts traced in random positions

c. Echoing outlines

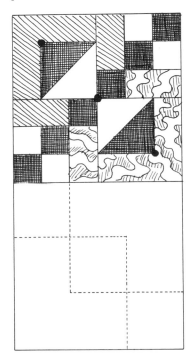

379. *Hayes' Corner* quilting pattern with hidden tacks in the pieced blocks at marked points

comforter effect. Since your first piece is a small one, you can safely experiment without fear of ruining a personal monument. Try not to leave unquilted spaces more than seven to ten inches square. Since the areas almost never *are* square, experimenting is the only way to learn how much quilting is enough for you. If you have hit on a pattern you like but are afraid some of the unquilted spaces are too large, anchor the batting in those areas with a few hidden tacks. Wash the piece once, and see how you like it. If it seems too loose and baggy for your taste, you can always add quilting or use quilting and knots or tufts in combination.

If the piece is a very large or formal affair, like the king-size bedspread *Hayes Corner,* you can still use a spare quilting design and simply resolve to have the quilt dry-cleaned. After all, if you paid $300 for an enormous and beautiful Nettle Creek bedspread you wouldn't expect to be able to wash it in the washing machine; for one thing, most washing machines aren't big enough to handle a piece that size. Surely your one-of-a-kind handmade masterpiece deserves as much care. You can bet your buttonhook that the pioneer woman who spent fourteen years piecing a *Blazing Star* out of scraps from her children's outgrown pinafores would have sent it to the dry cleaners too if she had had the chance.

MARKING

After you have worked out the design, spread out the quilt top on a hard, flat surface and draw the design directly on the patchwork with pencil or chalk. Be sure to mark the design on *before* you assemble the quilt, because after the soft batting is in place it will be difficult to make pencil marks without poking holes in the fabric. (However, you can mark with powder and a perforated pattern after the piece is assembled; some quilters prefer to mark each section just before they quilt to minimize smudging of the powder.)

ASSEMBLING THE QUILT

First, lay out the backing, right side down, on a bare table or floor—or on a carpet, if you must, but be careful not to baste the quilt to it. Carefully unroll and smooth the batting over the backing. Ease out wrinkles and center the layers, always handling the batting gently to avoid tearing it. Trim the edges of the batting even with the backing and save the scraps. (There's always something to do with extra batting.) Next, spread the top *carefully*, right side up, taking care not to disarrange the batting. Fuss with it gently until you are sure all three layers are smoothly and squarely on top of each other. There must be *no* wrinkles in any of the layers at this point, or they will be quilted into the piece for all time.

Next, pin-baste the three layers. Do it *very* carefully, row by row, using lots of pins and making sure you aren't shifting or wrinkling anything as you go. Unless the quilt is very small, you won't be able to use your hand under the quilt without bunching and shifting the work, so learn to pin with one hand, from the top. If it is a large quilt you will have to crawl across it to execute this step (make sure your knees are clean). You could thread-baste instead of pinning, working from the center to each corner and then making lots of diagonal lines between. It's what old-time quilters would have done, but I've never found it necessary, except for machine-quilting, so I advise you not to bother.

SETTING UP FOR QUILTING

After the quilt is thoroughly basted, you are ready to quilt it. You can use a quilting frame if you like (and, more to the point, if you have room). Traditional quilters feel that a frame is essential, but I think that's part habit, part horseradish. Of course you must have a frame if six of your friends are going to work along with you, and it is a convenience even if you are working alone, but it is not

380. Diagram for thread-basting

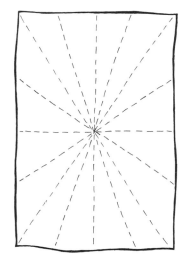

necessary. If you want one, I advise you to send for the inexpensive one offered by Sears Roebuck. It is beautifully made with hardwood stretchers, it has special wheel clamps that make the quilt easy to roll, and the top tilts. If you are good with tools and prefer to make your own, Stearns and Foster will send you a blueprint with complete instructions for about 35¢.

If you are using a frame, first cover the long stretchers with some heavy fabric like denim or mattress ticking. (The cut-off legs of abandoned blue jeans work nicely.) Tack the fabric firmly onto the stretchers with thumb tacks or a staple gun. Pin-baste one end of the quilt to one stretcher, and smoothly roll the entire quilt onto that stretcher. Try to keep the sides of the quilt parallel to the sides of the frame. If you are quite sure there were no wrinkles in the work before you set it in the frame, don't panic when the inside layer begins to crumple. It must in the nature of things because the inside is coiled more tightly than the outside, and the crumpling will disappear as the work unrolls. Pin the free end of the quilt to the opposite stretcher and turn the clamps to stretch the surface tight. The quilt should not sag and bag, but neither does it have to be so tense that you can't get a needle through it. Some quilters insist that the surface must also be stretched to the sides with strips of fabric, but again, I've never found it necessary, so I advise you not to bother.

If you are working without a frame, simply roll the quilt up lengthwise as smoothly and tightly as you can, leaving about two feet hanging out to begin work on. Place the roll on a table or ironing board with the free end hanging down, and sit on a chair in front of it. (Or you can sit cross-legged on a bed or on the floor with the work in your lap—just be careful to keep one hand behind the work so you won't sew it to your knee.) It is a good idea to weight the bulk with something heavy, such as a few telephone books, so it won't decide suddenly to unroll itself. You can see at once the advantage of this technique—if you're careful you can move the piece out of sight whenever you aren't working on it. With a frame you're stuck with it until the whole quilt is finished.

TO QUILT

Use a short, sharp needle, size 8–10. Larger than 8 makes too big a hole, smaller than 10 may break. I prefer 8 because it is easier to thread and it won't curve as easily, but some quilters insist you can't quilt properly without a curved needle. Just goes to show you, doesn't it? Try both and see which you like. Use quilting thread if you can get it; if you can't, use cotton-covered polyester thread, or cotton thread #50. If you have trouble with knotting, get a cake of beeswax at the notions store, run the threaded needle along it to coat the thread. Also try using shorter thread; you shouldn't be trying to quilt more than about 15″ at a time anyway.

Tie a small knot in one end of the thread and pass the needle through all three layers from back to front at a spot on a quilting line about a foot away from you. Tug gently till you feel the knot pop through the backing and lodge in the batting. Be careful not to pull it out the front. If it keeps popping through all three layers, try starting close to a seam where the seam margins will stop the knot. If the quilt pattern doesn't run near a seam, forget it and leave the knot on the back; the world won't blow up if a couple of knots show.

Take small running stitches along the lines marked. Traditional quilters say there should be 12 stitches to the inch, but I don't think it matters much as long as the stitches are even. Keep one hand behind the work, and try to graze your finger at each stitch to be sure the needle has gone through all three layers. Just be careful not to stab yourself; the judges at the county fair take a dim view of bloodstains on the backing. Try to make the stitches even on both sides (though you won't be able to at first). The length of each stitch will depend on your skill, and on the nature of the batting. Just do your best and remember that longer stitches stand more chance of snapping during the weight and strain of washing.

At first you may take only a stitch at a time; but quilting is really very fluid and easy and you should soon learn to take three or four stitches at a time before withdrawing the needle. For most people it is easiest to quilt toward the body, so start each line of stitching an arm's easy reach away from you, and quilt in. Quilting without a frame offers another advantage at this stage, since you can keep turning the work to quilt around curves and tricky angles, while on a frame you have to end the thread and approach from another direction.

A thimble on your middle finger will help you to work the needle up and down through the layers; even if you never use a thimble for other sewing, give it an honest try here. It really makes a big difference if you can get the hang of it. If the needle sticks, as it often does when you are working in hot weather or if one of your fabrics is tightly woven, it helps to dust talcum powder on the fingers and thumb of you needle hand.

To end each line of stitching, stop when you have one more stitch to make and tie a knot in the thread close to the quilt surface (a). Take the last stitch, giving a small tug to pull the knot through the top into the batting (b). Run the thread off into the batting underneath the next line of quilting to be sewn, so that the new stitches will secure the end of the thread. Bring the needle out the front and clip the thread.

If for any reason you can't get the knots to pop down through the top, finish the line with one or even two backstitches, running the thread off into the batting afterward. Backstitching will show, and we quilting fanatics try to make it so other quilt fanatics can't find our beginnings and our endings, but we are also very embarrassed when our quilting comes out in the wash, so you decide which is more important to you.

The instructions given above are for hand-

381. Ending a line of quilting.
a.

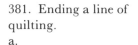

b.

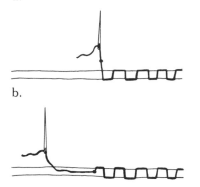

quilting on cotton quilts, but other kinds of quilts may demand other solutions. A silk quilt should be quilted with silk buttonhole twist, and a wool quilt will require a heavier needle and might be quilted with yarn. I have seen a handsome antique spread quilted with red yarn, in which the stitch lengths were varied to form a pattern within the quilting. This is feasible on a quilt that will not be washed, since there is less danger of long stitches snapping under pressure, and it is a good technique for a quilt top of heavy fabrics and especially for a quiltmaker who knows Morse code.

382. Yarn quilting pattern

MACHINE-QUILTING

It is also possible to quilt by machine, though to my mind, it is more trouble than it's worth on a large piece. If a presser foot is used to feed the work evenly through the machine, the quilt will have to be thread-basted so thoroughly beforehand to prevent the layers from shifting, that you might as well quilt by hand. You can use the machine set for embroidery and feed the work through manually instead, but it will take you some practice to keep the stitches even; remember that it is a large, heavy quilt you'll be hefting around, not a cambric hanky. If you look closely at a store-bought com-forter, you'll usually find that even a practiced worker with an industrial quilting machine makes a lot of stitches that are radically jerky and uneven. However, bear in mind that this may be all sour grapes on my part, since I don't happen to like machine-quilting myself. By all means try it if you want to; just be sure to baste *very* thoroughly first, and try at least one practice piece. Also remember that the smaller and lighter the piece of work, the easier machine-quilting will be. From pot holders to baby quilts, machine-quilting is a perfect alter-native. A special quilting foot which is available for about 40¢ from Singer is supposed to ride easily over three layers of material and has an adjustable

383. Lining basted to top with a grid of long running stitches

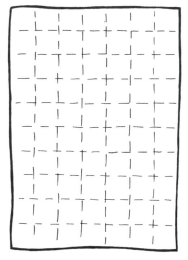

384. Pattern machine-quilted on

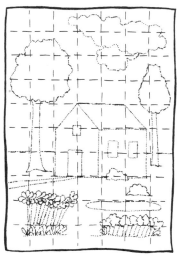

385. Back of the work (detail). Basting removed, slits cut in lining

guide gismo to help you make parallel lines without marking.

One really satisfactory method of machine-quilting is to quilt first and stuff and line the quilt afterward. This is especially suited to a pictorial appliqué quilt or to a modern all-white quilt in which the quilt stitching is itself the whole pattern. First, line the quilt top with a layer of muslin. Thread-baste the layers together in a grid; thread- or pin-baste the edges. Using a presser foot or the embroidery setting, top-stitch around the edges of the figures or patterns in the design. Remove the basting. On the back, make slits in the muslin lining within the lines of stitching, and stuff the pockets with quilt batting. Use more or less batting according to the amount of relief you want for each figure; variety in the amount of stuffing gives the quilt a special texture. Use a crochet hook to stuff nooks and crannies. If any hard-to-reach channels are formed by the stitching lines, do not slit the lining in those places. After the pockets are stuffed and closed, fill the channels with the method described for corded quilting, below. Catch-stitch slits closed, and back and bind the quilt as usual.

PADDED AND CORDED QUILTING

Some rare and beautiful old quilts were made with an English technique called padded work, on which the above method was based. The quilt, usually all-white, was assembled and elaborately quilted in the usual way. Then tiny holes were

386. Catch-stitch

poked in the back of the muslin beneath the portion of the design to be raised. Without breaking any threads, a heavy needle forced an opening through which wisps of batting were pushed up until the figure puffed up the desired amount. Then the threads were worked back together so that the hole disappeared. This was said to be the absolute ultimate in beautiful and difficult needlework, and I'm here to say amen to that. Beautiful it is, but not difficult—impossible.

I don't even like to think about the hours I've spent trying to cajole a single wisp of batting through holes of various sizes, without success. If you want to try it, good luck. The following is a compendium of the most likely-sounding instructions I could cull from every source I could find.

1. Use a loosely-woven backing to start with. I suspect homespun was easier to deal with in this process, though *They* say you can do it with muslin.

2. Make a hole in the backing where you want to insert padding, without breaking the threads of the weave. Start by inserting a darning needle, then move it in a circular motion to enlarge the hole it has made.

3. Insert a larger needle, perhaps a knitting needle, into the same hole, and enlarge again by moving the needle in a circular motion.

4. When the hole is slightly larger than the diameter of the knitting needle, insert tiny wisps of batting, poking it with the knitting needle into the space to be padded. Be careful not to stuff the area too full, for the batting will swell in the wash and could split the quilting stitches. (Better yet, if you succeed in stuffing it at all, plan to have the piece dry-cleaned.)

5. When you have finished stuffing, close the hole by working the threads back into place with the tip of a fine needle.

6. Grasp the work firmly at either side and stretch it, to make the padded area lie smooth.

Corded quilting, also called Italian or trapunto, is a raised effect made by inserting yarn or cotton cord through the backing into a narrow channel formed by lines of quilting. It is used by itself or together with padded quilting, for instance in a flower basket design which might have the leaves and blossoms padded and the narrow stems of the flowers raised with cord. It is easier to do than padded work, but unlike other kinds of quilting, it is not reversible. Lumps of yarn stick out of the back at various points, so the back is not really meant to be seen. It is also a purely decorative technique, since it provides no warmth. For both these reasons it is better suited to pillow covers than to quilts, though both padded and corded work have been popular for bedspreads in certain times and places.

To do corded quilting:

1. Cut a piece of muslin for lining the same size as the piece to be corded. Baste the lining to the top, wrong sides together.

2. Trace the design to be corded onto the lining. Then draw another line parallel to the first, about ¼″ distant. Quilt both lines neatly by hand or machine, taking care not to make the channel any narrower than you have drawn it.

3. Thread any embroidery or darning needle with white acrylic yarn (washable and colorfast) and insert the needle into the channel through the backing. Pass it through the channel as far as it can go, drawing the yarn along, then bring it up through the backing again; never let the needle pierce the other side of the work, which is the top (since you are working from the back).

4. Reinsert the needle almost in the same hole, and again pass it as far through the channel as it can reach. Every time you remove and reinsert the needle, you leave a little knot of yarn showing outside the work. This keeps the yarn from shifting later. Remove and reinsert the needle as often as you have to to turn any curves or corners.

5. Finish by simply bringing the yarn up out of the backing and cutting it off.

387. Yarn being worked into channel for corded quilting.

PRE-STUFFED UNITS

Instead of assembling a quilt in three full-sized sheets, you can assemble and stuff each patchwork unit separately as if it were a little pillow, then sew the units together for a finished, completely reversible quilt.

First, work out a pattern on graph paper using squares, triangles, or a variety of shapes (see drawings). Cut out two pieces of fabric for each shape you need, using a variety of prints and colors.

Start with two pieces of fabric, the same size but different colors. Match them right sides together and machine-stitch them together three-quarters of the way around the outside, as you would any pillow. Turn the pieces right side out and stuff with bits of dacron batting; slip-stitch the remaining free edge closed. Continue in this way until each unit of the patchwork has been made into a little stuffed pillow. If you like, you can machine-quilt each piece as it is finished.

Join the pieces to each other with a machine satin-stitch. You can also use a hand slip-stitch, but if you do you will have to sew each seam on the front and on the back to prevent them flapping open, as if on hinges.

Since each puff of patchwork had a different fabric on front and back, the finished quilt will be completely reversible, with a different arrangement of colors on each side.

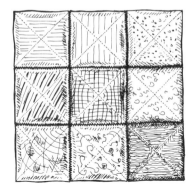

388. Squares pre-stuffed and quilted and joined with machine zig-zag

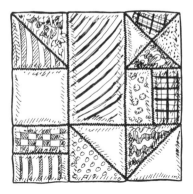

389. Pre-stuffed geometrics

10 QUILT PARTIES, GIFT QUILTS AND OTHER PROJECTS

There were two kinds of quilt parties in the old days. Everyone knows about the quilting bee; in the last few years such a mystique has grown up around the quilting process that some people talk as if it were the only interesting part of quilt-making, and the quilting bee the only legitimate quilting party. On the contrary, the really joyous special-occasion quilt parties were patchwork parties, where the guests together planned and stitched a quilt top. These were forerunners of our modern bridal and baby showers. In some locales the motif for a bridal quilt was an appliqué pattern drawn and cut by the potential bridegroom. In the 18th century a special quilting party was often held to celebrate a young man's coming of age; to celebrate anyone's special occasion, friends gave a Friendship Medley Surprise Quilt Party.

FRIENDSHIP MEDLEY SURPRISE QUILT PARTY

As the name implies, either the party or the quilt or both is a surprise to the guest of honor. All the other guests bring their scrap bags and their collection of patterns. In the old days, people saved all their quilt patterns like recipes, lending the good ones to their friends to copy, and when they saw a quilt in a new pattern they made up a sample block to refer to later. Once in a while in old attics, people come across whole trunks full of sample blocks waiting to be copied or shared. In these days people usually bring their quilt books and equipment for drafting patterns; the hostess provides material for the set, backing, and batting. They decide on a common size for the blocks, but each person chooses a different pattern, and helps her/himself to fabrics from everyone else's scrap bag. There is alleged to have been hot competition

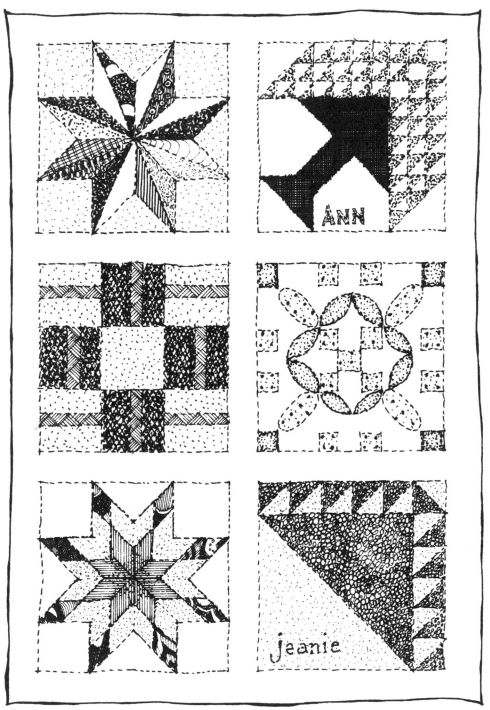

390. *Friendship Medley Surprise* quilt, 35″ × 50″. Made by Barbara Stockwell, Ann Meyer, Katherine Dalsimer, Joanne McGrath, Beth Gutcheon, and Jeanie Strouse

391. *Album* block

392. *Christian Cross* block

393. *Creeper Quilt*, detail

to see who could sew the trickiest pattern, and actually, since you're sewing by hand and only making one block, this is a good time to try something you mightn't ordinarily undertake. Besides, taking a little extra trouble is a way of expressing affection. Before setting the blocks together, each one signs her/his block with embroidery or indelible ink. The resulting gift may be striking, or a little uneven, or even a little ugly, but it's sure to be appreciated. The drawing shows such a quilt made in July 1972 for a baby present.

ALBUM QUILT

The album quilt was another popular presentation quilt. It was usually made for a friend who was moving west, or for an honored member of the community, like the minister, to whom everyone wished to be remembered. The quiltmakers agreed upon an album block, such as the two shown; then each person made up a block in her/his own choice of fabrics or combination of scraps and signed her name in the blank space. The quilt was assembled and quilted by one person or by all and presented at a party in honor of the recipient.

CREEPER QUILT

A patchwork is an ideal gift for a baby, since the variety of prints and colors is just what an infant's environment needs to provide interest and stimulation, to help him learn to focus his eyes and discern patterns and images. Any patchwork pattern is good, but a friend described to me a very special baby quilt called a creeper quilt. Designed with a neutral medallion surrounded by a border of intricate appliqué faces and figures, the creeper quilt works like a playpen; instead of bars, the border itself keeps the baby in place by keeping him interested.

To make a creeper quilt:

1. Cut a central panel about 45″ x 50″ in a solid color or light print.

2. Cut and apply a border in a dark color or

arresting print to be 10″ wide on all four sides of the central panel.

3. To make templates for the faces, first draw on graph paper four or five freehand faces just under 10″ high. Carefully cut out each part of each face, (eyes, nose, hair, and so on) and transfer the shapes to posterboard.

4. Cut out posterboard templates of each shape; do not add seam margins. At the same time cut one or two round or oval templates for the face shapes to which the features will be applied.

5. Using the templates wrong side up on the wrong side of the fabric, trace each shape several times using a different fabric each time if possible.

6. Cut out all shapes about ¼″ outside the traced line, for turning margins.

7. Prepare the pieces for appliquéing by pressing the turning margins to the inside.

Cut out enough pieces to assemble a few faces at a time. Use as many different fabrics as you can and try to vary your use of darks and lights so that some faces appear as the negative of others. When you have assembled the pieces into several faces in combinations that you like, sew them together using either hand-hemming or the machine zigzag stitch. If you like, stick a bit of batting under the eyes, nose, etc., before sewing them down, to put the features in relief.

When you have enough faces, arrange them around the border, experimenting to get the most various kinds of contrasts. If you want to you can intersperse the faces with little giraffes and bananas and so on. Baste and sew the figures in place, either with a blind stitch or machine zigzag. For quilting, simply outline the faces using several colors of thread. Quilt the central panel in a simple design, or use templates of fruits and animals for a random quilting pattern.

INITIAL QUILT

Children (not unlike regular people) have very strong feelings about property and ownership.

395. Initial Quilt

They like to feel that a thing is really specially made for them, not just passing through on the way from an older brother to the neighbor's daughter. With that in mind I designed this scrap quilt based on the letters of my son's name. This particular design is best for people named David, but most letters can be made up in simple patchwork elements; for things like Q's, it is always possible to add the hard parts with appliqué. Letters could also be alternated with plain blocks or blocks divided into rectangles or triangles, to add more design elements.

PLAYPEN LINER

Author and designer Ellen Morris suggested this idea for a quilted patchwork playpen liner. As I noted before, patchwork is ideal for an infant's environment, and it is especially useful here because playpen mats tend to get very grubby and because the manufacturers tend to print them with pink and blue bunnies, which are better out of sight.

1. Use the foam rubber mat that comes with the playpen or have a slab cut to size at a foam rubber store (look for one in the Yellow Pages).

2. Design and piece a panel of patchwork the size of the rubber square, plus about an inch all around (more, if the rubber is thicker). If you prefer you could use cotton printed to look like patchwork or other prints.

3. Cut lining and batting the same size as the top, assemble and baste the lining-batting-top, and quilt closely by hand or machine. Since this may have to be washed a couple of times a week rather than once a year like a quilt, it ought to be made to withstand a lot of wear.

4. Cut four rectangles of muslin or other fabric the length of the sides and 8″ or 10″ wide. Press a narrow hem on one long side of each rectangle; turn and press again to enclose raw edges and machine-stitch in place.

396. Playpen liner

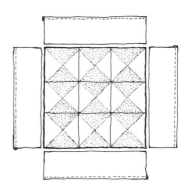

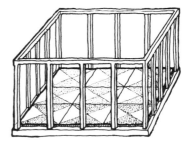

397.

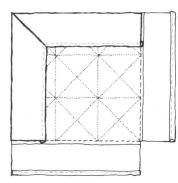

5. Sew the unhemmed edges to the patchwork, right sides together, through all layers, to secure the batting and the lining.

6. Turn the muslin pieces to the inside, miter the corners, and slip-stitch strongly by hand. The foam rubber mat can be inserted easily and removed easily when the cover needs washing.

PRESENTATION QUILT CASE

A large, fine presentation quilt is in most ways an ideal gift, for a gift of time and skill is to most people the most precious of all. If a quilt has a drawback, it is its shape and size; there seems to be no more dignified way to carry and store a beautiful quilt then wrapped in a plastic trash can liner or wadded into a shopping bag. To solve this problem, make a matching case for the quilt. (This was sometimes done for antique presentation quilts, especially if the recipient was going away and would have to carry the quilt on his/her travels, or if the quilt was so elaborate that it would only be brought out for special guests or special occasions.

1. To make one, fold the quilt as if for storage, and measure its dimensions.

399.

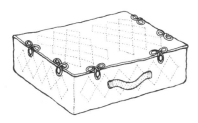

2. Cut or piece two large panels of fabric for the top and bottom of the case, and four for the sides, adding ½″ for seam margins around all sides. If you have enough, use one or more of the fabrics used in the quilt top.

3. Cut six lining pieces and six pieces of batting to match the top pieces.

4. For a handle, cut a strip of fabric 10″ long and 4″ wide.

5. Assemble the three layers of each panel, lining-batting-top, and quilt loosely by hand or machine. If possible, use a motif from the quilting pattern in the quilt, and only carry the stitching to within an inch of the edge.

400.

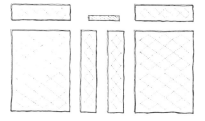

6. Fold the handle strip right sides together and sew the side, taking ½″ seam. Turn right side out and insert a strip of quilt batting 8″ long and

2″ wide, having the seam in the middle of the underside of the handle.

7. Turn in margins ½″ on each end of the handle and baste them together. Quilt loosely.

8. Position the handle in the center of the front panel on the right side, so that it humps up in the middle like the handle of a suitcase. Baste the ends of the handle in place and stitch through all layers, two or three lines of stitches on each end. This will be easiest and strongest if done by machine.

9. On all sides of all six pieces, trim the batting so that the edges of the fabric extend 1″ beyond it.

10. Sew the seams joining the four side panels, right sides together, through the *tops* only.

11. With four sides sitting in a square inside out, set the bottom panel in place. Baste the bottom panel to the side panels all around, through the outer or top layers of the case only. (Since the case is inside out at this point, the outside layers are all inside here.) Sew around all four sides as basted, taking ½″ seams.

12. Turn the work right side out. Baste the top panel to the back panel (the one opposite the handle), as above, with the outside layers right sides together, batting and lining layers free. Sew as basted, taking ½″ seam.

13. Inside the case turn in all the margins of the lining seams ½″, and slip-stitch the folds together, first the top and side seams, then around the bottom.

14. Turn in and whip together the free edges around the sides and top. For closings, use satin frogs from a notions store.

SCRAP BAG

If you have been saving scraps to make a quilt, or plan to start, or are just the sort who can't throw out two square inches of perfectly good material, you probably could use something to keep them in besides a paper bag from the supermarket. All the

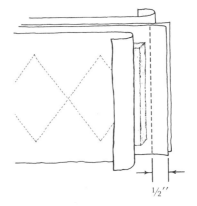

401. Sewing side seams through top layers only

½″

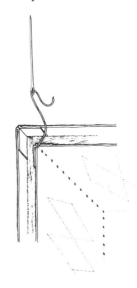

402. Slip-stitch inside seams

403.

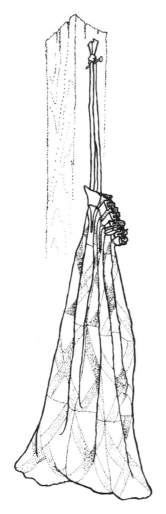

old quilt books talk about "your scrap bag" as if no decent home could be without one, so I thought the best response would be a bag not only for scraps, but from them. If you really are going to accumulate enough fabric for a quilt top, the scrap bag ought to be at least as large as a laundry bag; in fact, it could very well be used as a laundry bag.

1. Piece two panels of patchwork 24″ x 36″. Cut two layers of lining fabric to match.

2. Baste each panel of lining to one of patchwork, right sides together, and stitch around three sides. Turn each piece right side out; turn in and slip-stitch the fourth side closed.

3. Baste the lined panels right sides together, and stitch around the sides and bottom as shown, taking a ½″ seam. Leave 6″ free at the top sides. Turn the bag right side out.

4. Turn down the top edges of the bag three inches to the inside, and stitch them in place across the piece, leaving side edges free.

5. Make another seam 1½″ above the first, creating a channel for the draw string.

6. Cut a piece of soft, strong cord 46″ long or more. Knot one end of the string around a knitting needle or crochet hook, then use it to work the string through the channel on one side and back the other way on the other. Knot the ends of the cord securely.

404.

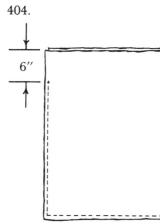

6″

405.

1½″   3″

8″

SEAT COVER FOR CHAIR OR STOOL

Quilted patchwork makes an excellent seat cover since it is its own padding and it can be removed and washed whenever someone spills gravy on it.

1. For a chair, place a large piece of paper on the seat top, and trim it until it fits exactly along all edges and around the legs, if necessary.

2. Trace and cut a piece of fabric the size of the paper, plus ½″ margin on all sides (but not in the angles around the legs).

Since the chair top is unlikely to be perfectly square, you could plan to cover the entire piece with crazy-piecing, using the techniques described for making a crazy-quilt top, or you could cut the piece from some solid color background material and hem onto it a pieced block or appliqué pattern.

3. When the top design is completed, cut lining and batting pieces the same size as the seat top. Assemble and quilt the three layers to within an inch of the edge.

4. Measure and cut or piece a length of fabric 5″ wide and long enough to extend around the front and both sides of the chair. This will give a border 4″ wide plus ½″ margins; it may be crazy-pieced (if the seat is) or a border pattern such as *Saw Tooth* or *Lightning*, or a solid piece to match the background of the seat. For the back, cut or piece a similar panel 5″ wide, and as long as the back minus the legs.

5. Cut the lining and batting pieces the same size as these pieces, assemble, and quilt to within 1″ of the edge. Attach the two border pieces to the seat by basting the *tops only*, right sides together, and sewing all around, taking a ½″ seam.

6. On the inside of the work, turn in the lining margins of this seam and slip-stitch them together.

7. Using narrow bias strips of fabric or pre-cut bias tape

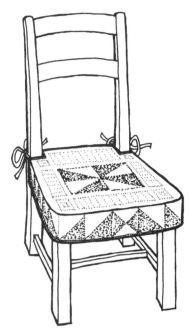

407.

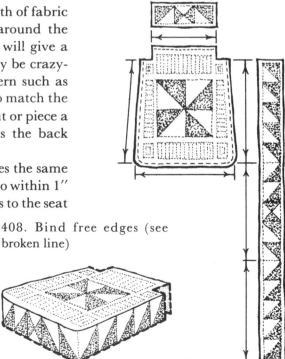

408. Bind free edges (see broken line)

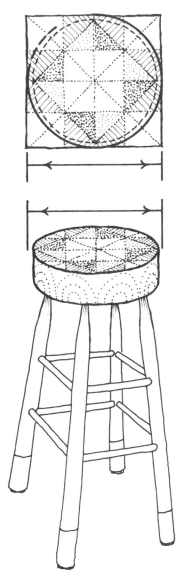

409.

from a notions store, bind the bottom edge of the border along the front and sides, around the space left for the legs, and across the back.

8. For strips to tie the seat in place, cut four ribbons of bias tape 12″ long, or make tapes: cut four strips of fabric 1″ wide and 12″ long. Turn in and press ¼″ hem on each side. Fold the strip down the center having the hemmed edges together, and whip or top-stitch the edge closed.

Sew a ribbon in each corner of the angles formed for the chair legs, and tie them behind the legs in a tight bow to hold the seat in place.

To make a cover for a round stool:

1. Measure the diameter of the seat and piece a square block as wide as the seat plus ½″ on all sides. (Make templates with ½″ margins instead of ⅜″.)

2. Tie a string around a pencil. Hold the end of the string firmly in the exact center of the block and place the pencil point at the center of one side on the edge of the margin, not on the seam line.

3. Draw a complete circle, having the arc touch the edge of the margin at the exact center of each side. Cut out the circle on the line, and cut lining and batting to match. Assemble the layers and quilt to within an inch of the edge.

4. Cut a piece of plain fabric, or piece a strip of patchwork, 5″ wide and as long as the circumference of the circle, plus 1″ (4″ of patchwork, plus ½″ margins).

5. Quilt the strip to within 1″ of the edge, and trim the batting 1″ from the edges on all sides of all pieces.

6. Sew the top layer of the border to the top layer of the seat, basting thoroughly first to ensure a smooth seam, and leaving ½″ margins.

7. On the inside, turn in and slip-stitch the ½″ margins of the lining seams.

8. Turn in and slip-stitch both top and lining margins at the seam joining the two ends of the border.

410.

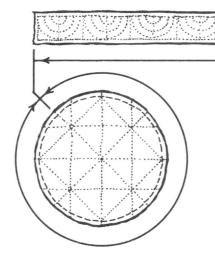

9. Turn in and slip-stitch the bottom edge of the border, or bind it with bias tape.

SEWER'S POCKET

For people who like to always have their work near them and yet prefer not to have their arms loaded down with work bags, consider an old-fashioned quilted sewer's pocket. Quilting is the perfect material for all kinds of sewing equipment because it is strong enough not to be damaged by sharp, jangling scissors, as a single layer of fabric would be, and the padding allows the material itself to act as a needle paper and a pin cushion.

A sewer's pocket is simply a small sewing kit that is tied around the waist with ribbons and works like a pocket. To make the traditional one shown:

1. Make 12 patchwork squares each 4″, plus ⅜″ margins.

2. Join six squares as shown for the back panel; cut lining and batting to match, and quilt to within ¾″ of the edge.

3. Join the squares for the front into two vertical strips of three squares each. Cut lining and batting to match, and quilt each strip to ¾″ from the edge.

411. Sewer's pocket

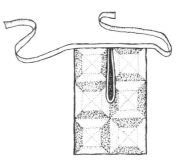

412.
a. Back panel b. Front strips

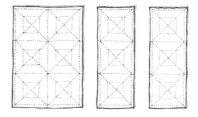

413. Bound placket

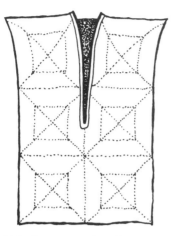

414. Baste top closed

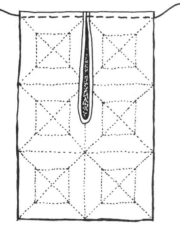

415. Waist ribbon cuffed and stitched over pocket top

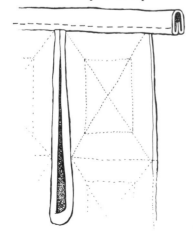

4. Trim batting in ¾″ from the edge along the sides and bottom of all pieces.

5. To join the front, place the strips of squares right sides together and sew a 6″ seam through *tops only* from the center of the panel to the bottom, leaving the top 6″ free for the placket (opening) of the pocket.

6. On the inside of the piece, turn in and slip-stitch the margins of the lining, again leaving the top 6″ free.

7. Join the front and back by placing them right sides together and stitching together *tops only* along sides and bottom.

8. Turn in and slip-stitch bottom and side seams of the lining. Turn the pocket right side out.

9. With purchased tape or bias stripping, bind the placket. Then baste the top edges of the pocket together.

10. Cut a strip of binding material for a ribbon to tie around the waist. The length will depend upon the girth of the wearer, but 60″ ought to be ample for most. If you are not using prepared tape, cut the strip 1½″ wide and turn in and press a hem ¼″ wide on each side.

11. Place the pocket in the center of the strip. Cuff the strip over the top of the pocket as shown, enclosing all raw edges and having the hems of the strip on the inside. Baste in place.

12. Starting at one end of the waist ribbon, top-stitch the hemmed edges of the strip together, continuing across the pocket through all layers, and to the end of the ribbon. Turn in and secure the ends of the ribbon.

PINCUSHION OR BABY BALL

Over the last few centuries patchworkers have experimented with every conceivable geometric shape, and they discovered that the most intractable by far was the pentagon. There is no way to make pentagons lie flat, and 12 make themselves into a ball (actually, a dodecahedron). Under the circumstances, there seemed to me nothing for it

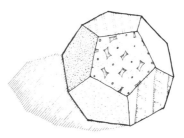

but to fashion this endless surface of pentagons to stick pins in. Made on a large scale, the same device is a perfect toy to roll and squash and toss around.

1. The basic pentagon for this is a plane with five equal sides and all angles 72°. Make a window template of a pentagon, using a protractor or a tracing of the drawing given here to help you make the angles.

Make the sides about 1½″ for a pincushion, 4″ for a baby's ball, and each angle 72°. Add a ⅜″ margin all around and carefully cut out the center of the template on the seam line.

2. Mark and cut 12 pentagons of fabric, marking on the wrong side of the fabric and using pencil or chalk for the seam lines.

3. Take the cut-out center portion of the template, place it within the seam lines on the wrong side of one of the fabric pentagons, and press all margins to the inside over the cardboard. Make sure to make the corners neat and sharp, and repeat for the rest of the pieces.

4. Seam the pieces together with slip-stitches through the folded and pressed edges, sewing from the corners outward as you set in each new piece. When 11 are joined, stuff the piece with wisps of batting using a knitting needle or crochet hook to poke the stuffing into all the corners. The shape should be firm but not taut, for the batting tends to swell during washing and might break the stitches. Slip-stitch the last pentagon in place.

417. Pentagon

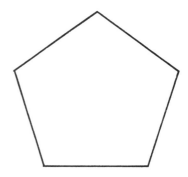

COMFORTER COVER

If you have an old comforter in the house, too ratty to use and too useful to throw out, you can restore it with a patchwork cover made like a huge pillow case.

1. Make a patchwork top to the dimensions of the comforter; be sure to measure generously to allow for the puffy batting.

2. Cut a lining the same size as the top, and another piece of lining for a cuff, measuring about 2″ by the width of the top.

418. Top

419. Lining (hemmed)

421. Cuff stitched and basted
to top

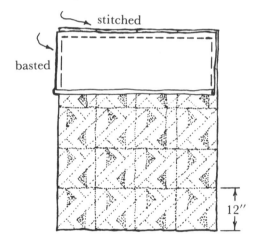

stitched

basted

12″

3. Turn a narrow hem to inside on one long edge of the cuff. Turn in again to enclose the raw edge and stitch in place.

4. Baste the free edges of the cuff to one end of the patchwork top, right sides together, and seam as shown.

5. At the top edge of the lining, turn in and stitch a hem as you did on the cuff.

6. With the cuff still basted to the right side of the top, center and baste the lining over the top, right side inside, and sew around the sides and bottom of the work, joining in the cuff on the sides.

7. Turn the case right side out, insert the comforter at the top, and turn the cuff to the lining side to secure the opening. (It's like a giant Glad Bag.)

420. Cuff (hemmed)

PILLOWS

If a very complex block appeals to you, but it has so many pieces that a quilt top would take you forever, the perfect solution is to make one block and turn it into a pillow.

1. For a knife edge pillow, piece any block from 12″ to 20″ in diameter. Cut a lining piece the same size, or piece another block in the same or a different pattern. Quilting serves no functional purpose in a pillow top, but you can also back and quilt the top before assembling the pillow, if you wish to emphasize the design.

2. Place the quilted or unquilted panels right sides together and sew three sides.

3. Clip the corner seam margins diagonally and turn the work right side out.

4. Stuff the pillow with dacron batting and slip-stitch the last side closed.

A pillow stuffed with dacron batting may be machine-washed in warm water as long as it is then thoroughly tumble-dried in a dryer. (It is difficult to get a pillow thoroughly dried in any other way. Cotton batting is not good for pillow stuffing because it takes longer to dry, and if batting is damp too long there is danger of mildew.)

BACKING A NEEDLEPOINT PILLOW

Since backing a pillow is so easy it has always seemed a shame to me that talented needlepersons spend months on an intricate and original needlepoint pillow top and then pay a fortune to have the Woman's Exchange back it with lilac plush just like everyone else's needlepoint pillow. A handsome patchwork block makes a really special and original backing for a needlepoint pillow. Since the pillow will not be washed, you are free to use silks and velvets for an elegant finish.

1. Piece a block the size of the needlepoint work, plus seam margins. If the needlepoint is a rectangle or other odd shape, add borders to the square to fill out the dimensions, or cut a muslin piece the size of the needlepoint plus margins and build upon it Victorian crazy patchwork in silks and velvets, with embroidery stitching in contrasting colors of silk thread.

2. Place the finished pieces right sides together having the needlepoint on top. Stitch around three sides on or just inside the outermost row of needlepoint, so no canvas will show at the seam. Trim the canvas to match the margins of the patchwork. Trim margins diagonally at the corners. If you like, you can bind the edges of the canvas with narrow masking tape.

3. Turn the pillow right side out and stuff it with batting, taking care to fill all the corners. Turn in the free edge and slip-stitch closed.

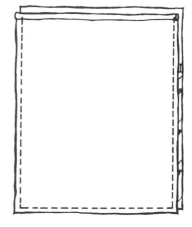

422. Sewing three sides of lining and top, joining in cuff at sides

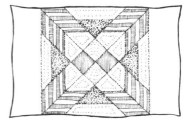

423. Pieced pillow

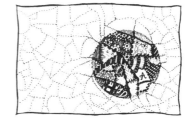

424. Crazy pillow

425. *Lover's Knot* pillow

426. Monogram pillow

427. Empire dress with quilted skirt

CORDED PILLOWS

Corded quilting, described in the preceding chapter, is an effective technique, but not especially well suited to bedcoverings because it provides no warmth and because it is not reversible—the back is definitely not meant to show. However, it is perfectly suited to pillow tops. Here are two ideas for corded pillows, one in the traditional *Lover's Knot* pattern, the other a monogram pillow for a gift.

For the first, follow the directions for corded quilting (page 198). Trace the *Lover's Knot* pattern onto the back of the lined pillow top, and be careful not to pierce the top layer as you work the needle in and out of the backing. The pattern will show up best on solid color. When the cording is finished, sew the decorated top to the pillow back around three sides, and finish as above.

For the monogram pillow, first appliqué the monogram to the pillow top, then baste the lining in place and quilt parallel lines of stitches ¼″ apart on the letters, using thread to match either the letters or the background. Join the top right sides together to the backing of the pillow around three sides, turn right side out, and finish as above.

CLOTHES

Many techniques described in this book can be used for making or decorating clothes as well as quilts. The Chinese have worn quilted clothing for centuries; they may in fact have invented quilting. Quilting is popular now for such garments as Chinese-style Mandarin evening jackets or evening skirts. However, the padding is not really necessary for warmth and it has the disadvantage of making all but the most slender look distressingly square.

The best design I have seen for a ladies' quilted garment is this empire cocktail dress. The high waistline moots the problem of boxy hips and the vertical quilting allows the skirt to move gracefully with the wearer. To make it, choose any simple empire dress pattern. For the bodice, choose a soft, supple fabric like panne velvet or silk jersey; for the skirt, use any smooth fabric like silk or elegant Liberty cotton; don't use velvet or velour for the skirt, for the quilting stitches would be lost in the nap and the extra bulk would be more than even this design could take.

1. Cut the bodice of the dress as directed by the pattern, and cut top, backing, and lining pieces for each section of the skirt.

2. If you are going to quilt by hand, mark the skirt pieces carefully with a yardstick and a chalk pencil on the top of the fabric. For the front, fold the piece in half vertically and press in a crease from center top to bottom. Then measure and mark vertical lines parallel to the crease about an inch apart.

3. For the back pieces, measure and mark parallel to the straight edge of the center seam. Assemble, baste, and quilt all the skirt pieces as usual, taking care not to extend the quilting beyond the seam lines to the margin.

If you prefer, this is a perfect time to use machine-quilting. Press the crease in the center, as above. Assemble the layers and baste thoroughly. Machine-quilt the crease, beginning and ending ⅝″ from the edge of the work. Adjust the guide on the quilting foot to one inch, and quilt vertical lines parallel to the first one. Quilt the back pieces in lines parallel to the straight edge of the center seam.

4. Trim the batting ⅝″ in from the edges all around all pieces. Sew the side seams of the skirt by joining the *tops only,* right sides together. Sew the back seam, *tops only,* from hem to the mark for the bottom of the zipper. On the inside, turn in and slip-stitch the lining at these seams.

5. Assemble the bodice according to the pattern directions, then sew it, right sides together, to the top only of the upper edge of the skirt. On the inside, turn in the lining at the upper edge of the skirt and hem it to the seam.

428. Appliqué skirt
a. Front

b. Back

6. To insert the zipper: turn in and press the ⅝″ margin on both the top and lining layers of the zipper opening, in the skirt, and on the bodice. Baste the zipper in place, having the tape *between* the top and lining edges of the skirt opening. Sew the zipper in place by hand or machine, joining all layers.

7. Try on the dress for length. If it needs to be shortened, trim to within ½″ of the desired length and turn in and baste the top and lining. Top-stitch the hem through all layers to secure the cut lines of quilting.

If the length is correct, simply turn in and slip-stitch the top and lining margins. If it must be lengthened, add a decorative binding in a contrasting color wide enough to achieve the desired length. Follow directions for applying binding to a quilt (page 169).

APPLIQUÉ SKIRT

Appliqué is a decorative technique used for many more things than quilts. Cambridge artists Judy and Todd McKie use it to make banners and murals in felt, applying figures to the background with a machine satin-stitch.

Judy uses the same technique to decorate evening skirts. To make the one shown:

1. Choose a simple A-line skirt pattern and a solid background fabric such as light wool (woven, not knit).

2. Cut out the skirt according to the pattern.

3. To make the design, lay a sheet of tracing paper over the skirt piece and sketch lightly with a blunt-tip felt marker (a Magic Marker). When the sketch is completed, cut out each figure and use it as a pattern to trace and cut figures out of various colors of felt.

If you draw well, you might prefer to dispense with the preliminary sketch and draw figures without patterns directly on felt. You can then lay the cut-out figures on the skirt pieces and fiddle around with them until they make an effect you like.

The felt pieces are cut directly on the seam line; no margins for turning under are necessary, because felt doesn't ravel and the satin stitches will cover the edges.

4. Pin-baste the felt pieces to the skirt sections, right side up on the right side of the fabric. Shift the pieces until the pattern pleases you, then satin-stitch them in place, or use a blanket-stitch if you are sewing by hand. Assemble the skirt according to the directions on the pattern.

CRAZY-PIECED SKIRT

A unique and beautiful evening skirt can also be made with Victorian crazy-piecing, and this is a great way to get rid of all your husband's old silk ties.

Choose a simple A-line skirt pattern; a pinched or gathered waistline would be hard to handle and boxy-looking around the hips. Cut out all pattern pieces in muslin and cover the right side of the pieces with silks, satins, velvets, and wool challis in crazy-piecing as described in the construction chapter. Embroider the seams by hand or machine.

The waistband can be crazy-pieced too, or if your waist is already thick enough, use a strip of silk or a wide grosgrain ribbon. Assemble the skirt according to pattern directions, and finish by trimming the hem to the desired length and binding with a strip of silk or grosgrain to match the waistband.

VESTS

Regular piecework can be used in almost any garment, provided you are willing to make yards of piecework only to cut it up again. The only proviso is that the garment should be lined so that the seam margins of the patchwork (as well as the seam margins of the garment) cannot shed, fray, or ravel. A man's or woman's reversible vest is a perfect

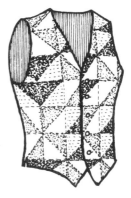

429. Man's vest

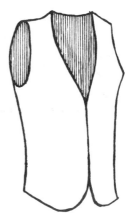

430. Loose vest

431. Bolero

project for patchwork because it is self-lined and if it is made with two different patchwork patterns it will serve as two garments in one.

You can buy a vest pattern in the appropriate size, or if you have (or can borrow) one of the loose-fitting kind without darts, you can make your own pattern by tracing the front and back pieces and adding a ⅝″ seam margin. If you use a purchased pattern, omit pockets, as they will only detract from the patchwork.

Lay the back and front pattern pieces end to end, as shown, to see how large a piece of patchwork you will need. The piece must be as long as the two pieces and at least twice as wide, because it will be folded in half for cutting. Design and piece two sheets of patchwork in two different patterns to the desired size. They will probably need to be about 3′ x 4′ and should have blocks either 8″ or 10″.

432.
a. Top pattern

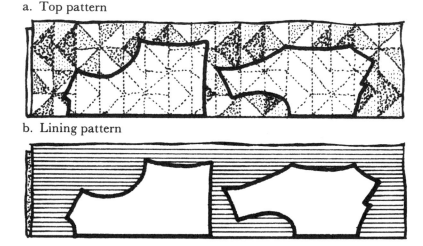

b. Lining pattern

When each sheet is pieced and pressed, fold it in half and lay out the two pattern pieces for cutting. Position the center line of the back on the fold, so that the back will be cut in one piece.

To assemble:

1. Match a front piece of the top pattern, right sides together, to the front piece of the lining. Sew them together around the armhole and from the shoulder to the corner of the lower edge, as shown.

2. End stitches at the black dots, and leave the sides free. Repeat for the other front pieces. Clip all curves and turn the pieces right side out. Press.

3. Next, make a sandwich, with the front pieces between the two backs. Lay out the lining back, right side up. Thread-baste the two fronts to it at shoulders and sides, matching patchwork patterns together, as shown. Remember that the raw edges of the back will extend beyond the finished edges of the fronts by ⅝″.

Place the top back, right side down, over all and match the edges of the backs. Baste all around as shown, joining in the front pieces at sides and shoulders. Make sure the fronts are *not* basted in at armholes and neck and across the bottom. Baste only about 5″ across the bottom at each side. Before stitching, slide your hand inside at the free bottom edge and check to be sure that the fronts are free at the armholes, neck, and bottom edge. Stitch as basted.

4. Clip curves and turn the vest right side out; press. Turn in the free bottom edge and slip-stitch closed. Finish with buttonholes and a row of buttons inside out, or a single hook and eye, or omit closings.

GIFTS—POTHOLDERS, WALL HANGINGS, COASTERS, MATS AND HOT PADS

For small, quick patchwork gifts, two small blocks can be made into reversible potholders.

1. Piece two blocks the same size, 6″ or 8″ square, but with different patterns.

2. Cut a piece of batting the same size as the blocks and assemble the three layers with the blocks right sides together, the batting on top.

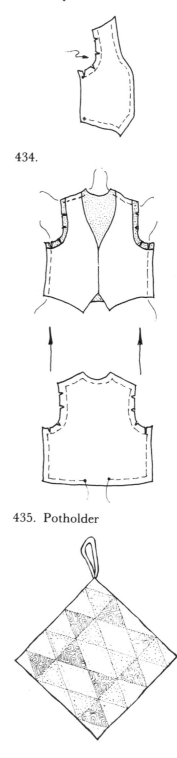

433. Clips

434.

435. Potholder

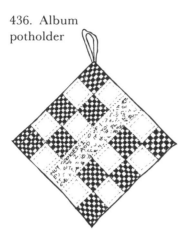

3. Sew by hand or machine around three edges. Trim the batting close to the seam; turn right side out.

4. For a loop by which to hang the potholder, cut a strip of fabric used in the pattern, 3½″ by 1″. Press in a narrow hem on each side of the strip; fold lengthwise, having hems together, and top-stitch the open edge closed.

5. Slip-stitch the fourth side of the potholder closed, joining in the raw ends of the loop in one corner. Quilt by hand or machine.

RECIPE POTHOLDER OR WALL HANGING

If you have a special recipe you want to give someone you could make this potholder from two album blocks and write the recipes in the blank spaces with indelible ink. Or, design a patchwork wall hanging with a space to write in, and loops in two corners to hang it by.

COASTERS

Quilted coasters are another gift idea. You can make a set quickly using two hexagons of fabric and one of batting for each coaster. Assemble in this order: batting, lining (right side up), and top (right side down).

Sew the hexagons around five sides. Trim the batting and clip corner margins diagonally; turn the pieces right side out, slip-stitch the free edge, and quilt by hand or machine.

437. Kitchen wall hanging

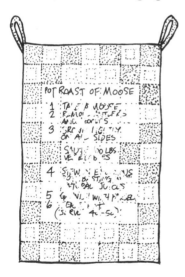

438. Coaster

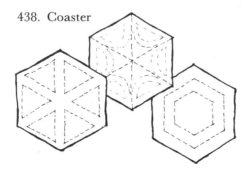

222

MATS AND HOT PADS

Quilted patchwork place mats and hot pads are also handsome gifts and are made the same way as coasters. A set could be made with each mat the same block but a different combination of colors, or each block different. Or use large pieced hexagons, or the appliqué pattern *Dresden Plate*.

439. Place mats

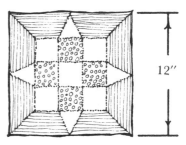

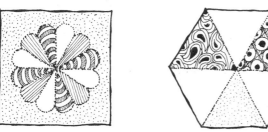

BABY BLOCKS

For a baby gift, consider foam rubber patchwork blocks. You can roll them and build them just like regular blocks, but if you prefer, you can squash them up and stuff them into your mouth.

At the foam rubber store, which you will find listed in the Yellow Pages, have blocks cut about 2″ square. Cut squares of fabric 2″ plus seam margins, six for each block. Use a different fabric for each side of the block, and if you like you can appliqué numbers or letters onto the squares before you assemble.

1. Sew together three squares to form three sides of the block.

2. Set in the top and bottom squares to make an open-ended cube; then place the rubber block inside. Fold in the seam margins even with the edges of the foam block all around.

3. Center the last square over the opening and secure with a straight pin stuck into the foam. With a pin, slide the raw edges under the folded edges of the adjoining pieces and slip-stitch the sides closed.

440.

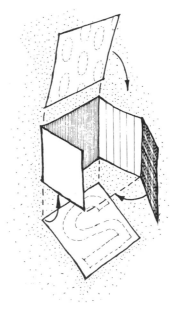

223

441.

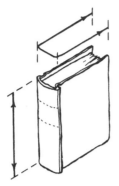

442.
a.

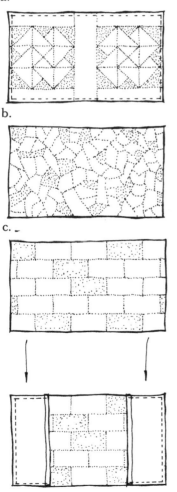

b.

c.

BOOK COVERS

To protect cookbooks, which tend to grow grimy from spattered wine sauce and cooky batter, you might be interested in this idea for a quilted book cover. It can be washed and the inside flaps hold recipe cards and clippings, and it can also be used to conceal paperbacks of a lurid nature when reading on the subway.

1. With a tape measure, measure the closed volume from edge to edge, as shown, and the height of the book along the spine.

2. Make a patchwork rectangle in these dimensions in one of the following ways: a) Make two blocks with borders and a strip between, as shown; b) Use crazy quilting; c) Use a one-patch design, like *Brickwork*.

In planning, be sure to figure an extra ½″ or so to account for the extra bulk of three layers and to include seam margins.

3. Cut a lining and piece of batting the same size as the piecework; cut two flap ends of muslin or lining fabric the height of the book plus margins 4″ wide.

4. Assemble the three layers as usual and quilt by hand or machine to within an inch of the edge.

5. Turn under a narrow hem along one long side of each flap and sew it in place.

6. Baste the three free sides of the flaps to the top, right sides together, and sew as shown through flaps and *top only*. Trim the corners diagonally and trim the batting in from the edge 1″ (or a little less) all the way around.

7. Turn the seam margins of top and lining (and flaps) to the inside and slip-stitch. Turn flap ends to the inside and insert the book.

TRAVELING GAME BOARD

If you are thinking of a gift for your circuit-riding minister or for friends going west in a wagon train, or if you yourself are a frequent visitor in

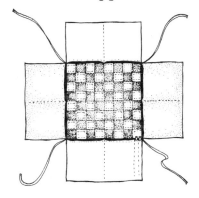

homes where all the decks have only 51 cards, consider this traveling game board. The board itself is quilted patchwork, and the extension pieces are pockets for chess people, checkers, cards, score pads, and pencils, and there's plenty of room for a set of dominoes, or mah-jong or scrabble tiles, or poker chips.

First make a square template for the checkerboard. The standard size is 2¼″ square, but Bobby Fischer prefers 2⅛″ and Lewis Carroll about ⅓ of an acre; you can adjust the size to suit yourself, but I'll use 2¼″ here for an example.

1. Make a square posterboard template 3″ on each side (2¼″ plus ⅜″ seam margins).

2. Cut 32 light squares and 32 dark. Use white and black, or a light solid and a dark print or any such combination as long as there is a high contrast between them.

3. Sew these row by row into a checkerboard with eight squares on a side. As in all patchwork, take care with the seam joints.

4. Cut a layer of backing and of batting the size of the assembled checkerboard. Baste the three layers as for a quilt, and quilt; I suggest outlining all alternate squares (i.e., all the squares of one color), which will result in a quilted checkerboard on the reverse side.

The checkerboard should measure 18¾″ on each side—18″ plus ⅜″ margin on each side. Be sure to measure, and adjust the dimensions of the extension pieces if necessary, but for the moment, let's assume that it came out the way it was supposed to.

5. Cut four rectangles, two from each color in the checkerboard, measuring 19½″ by 19¼″. On each, turn in and press the ¼″ to the wrong side for a hem and stitch it in place.

6. Fold each piece right sides together to form a pocket 9″ deep, as shown. This will leave an inch free above the pocket. Baste, and stitch the sides as shown, leaving ⅜″ margins on each side. Clip

444.

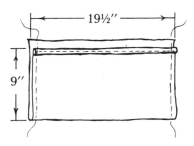

445. Pocket turned right side out; hem presses down

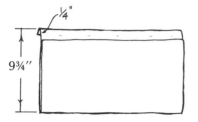

1/4"

9¾"

18¾"

446.

3/8"

447. Folded for traveling

diagonally at the corners and turn pocket right side out.

7. On the free edge of the extension above the pocket, turn a ¼" hem to the wrong side, and press.

8. Use the edge to form a binding for the checkerboard as follows: baste the hemmed edge of the extension piece over the seam margin on *top* of the checkerboard, having the hem exactly on the seam line. Turn the extension piece under so that the back of the pocket is against the back of the checkerboard.

Sew a seam along the edge of the board leaving exactly ⅜". This will simultaneously join the pocket to the board and bind the edge of the quilting. Only be sure you aren't stitching the pocket closed in the process. Repeat for the other three extension pieces, placing matching pockets across the board from each other.

9. Divide one pocket with a line of stitching down the middle to form two pockets for two packs of cards. On the opposite pocket sew a line of stitches ½" from the side of the pocket and another ½" from the first to form two slots for pencils. If you like, divide this pocket again to hold a bridge pad, or leave the space free for miscellaneous items like dental floss, pretzels, or spare change—whatever you need to play whatever you play. The other pockets are for checkers and chess people respectively, and can be divided in half to separate light and dark pieces.

10. To finish, sew a tie in each corner, covering any exposed edges of quilting if necessary. Make ties from fabric by cutting a strip 1" wide, turn in and press ¼" hem on each side. Fold the strip in half lengthwise with the hems together and stitch closed.

Fold the extension pieces over the board for traveling the way people fold closed cardboard boxes, i.e., with each flap under the adjacent one on one side and over the adjacent one on the other. Secure by tying the ties diagonally, as shown.

PATCHWORK NEEDLEWORK
OR TOTE BAGS

A quilted bag can be made in a small size for use as a knitting or needlepoint bag—as I said before, quilted fabric is ideal for such a purpose because it can itself be used as a needlepaper or pincushion and it isn't much damaged by scissors and knitting needles and so on. However, I urge you to make a gigantic shoulder bag, for the following reasons. First, a shoulder tote bag enables you to carry up to three tons of books, groceries, etc., and still have both hands free. This is a great convenience to anyone, but if you are regularly accompanied by a baby in a carrier or stroller it is a necessity. I have yet to discover how other parents get anything home, unless they have everything delivered.

But the most important consideration is that when you have your own bag you don't need to take bags from everyone else—paper bags and wrapping from the drug store, three layers of shopping bags every time you go to the grocery store, mod gear plastic bags from the shoe store. They kill green trees to make those bags, and you bring them home by the dozen, use for twenty minutes and then thrown away, and the next day you bring home a dozen more. You have to be bothered to ball them up and throw them away, and someone else has to be bothered to burn them or haul them to the dump, and then we are all bothered by the mountains of needless waste and the fumes and noxious gases and ashes of paper and plastic endlessly burning. How much more responsible it is to take an hour or two to make a bag that will last for years and do the work of all the others, and how fitting to make it patchwork.

Patchwork has always been inspired by a respect for the environment; its spirit is economy, not only of goods and money but also of our natural resources. People tried to throw nothing away that could conceivably be recycled, and products that could be used only once and thrown away were

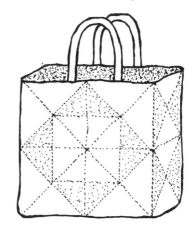

448. Needlework bag

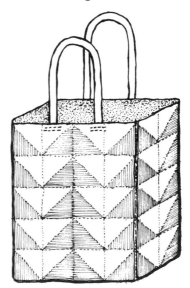

449. Tote bag

227

450.

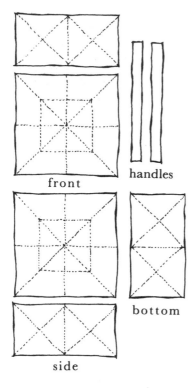

front

handles

bottom

side

451.

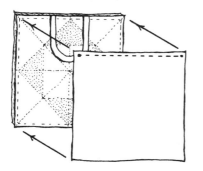

thought of as the ultimate in foolishness rather than as a status symbol in a society that reveres conspicious consumption. Cheap cotton was used instead of paper to package such goods as sugar and tobacco. It doesn't take fifty years to grow another cotton plant; and the fabric would not be thrown away; it was, of course, saved for patchwork. Many scraps in old quilts bear legible brand names and advertising.

To make a needlework bag:

1. Piece two blocks 12″ square for the main panels. From a fabric used in the patchwork, cut three panels 12¾″ x 4¾″ for sides and bottom. Cut lining and batting pieces to match all five pieces.

2. For handles, cut two strips of fabric 15″ x 4¾″. Fold the handle pieces in half lengthwise, right sides together, and sew the long side, taking a ⅜″ seam. Cut two strips of batting 15″ x 1¾″. Turn the handles right side out and press, having the seams down the center of the underside. With a knitting needle or crochet hook, work the batting through the handles. Quilt.

3. Assemble the main panels of the bag in this way: lay out the batting piece, then the pieced block, right side up. Position the handles as shown, with each end equidistant from the center and top sides against the right side of the patchwork. Baste. Lay the lining piece wrong side up over all; stitch by hand or machine across the top, joining the handles and ending the stitches at the seam line on either side. Turn the lining to the back and repeat for the other panel.

4. Assemble two side panels thus: batting, top (right side up), lining (right side down). Stitch across the top to within ⅜″ of the edges; turn right side out. Assemble the bottom panel in the usual way, first lining (wrong side up), then batting, then top.

5. By hand or machine, quilt all five pieces to within ¾″ of all unfinished edges. (Quilt all the way to the finished edge, if desired.) Trim batting ¾″ around all free edges.

6. For a pocket for scissors, stitch-holders, etc., cut a piece of fabric 5″ square. Turn in and press ¼″ hem all around. Stitch the hem in place across one side. As shown, baste the pocket to the wrong side of one square panel, having the stitched hem at the top. Blind-stitch the pocket only to the lining layer of the panel.

7. Join the sides of the bag as shown, having the pieces right sides together, all the finished edges at the top, sewing a ⅜″ seam through top layers only.

8. Set in the bottom panel before sewing the last side seam. Baste main and side panels to the bottom, right sides together, through tops only around all four edges, and sew. Baste and sew the last side seam through top layers only.

453. Order of joining

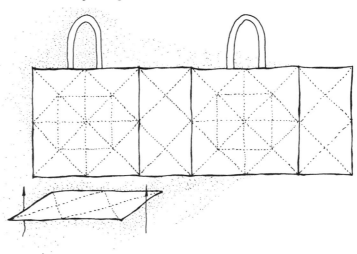

9. With the bag still wrong side out, turn in all margins of all lining and seams and firmly slip-stitch closed. Finis.

A larger bag, made the same way but with a stronger finish to the seams, is ideal for an informal overnight bag, picnic basket, or for toting diapers and baby rubble. But for really heavy-duty hauling (books or groceries) you need stronger fabric than the usual cotton. This is the perfect place to use printed denims and sailcloth. Make patchwork panels in the dimensions given below and cut lining pieces of soft muslin, but omit batting and quilting. Follow instructions for applying handles and the change-pocket, and join panels as described below or with French seams—a heavy seam with a parallel line of top-stitching ¼″ away to strengthen the seam and secure seam margins. (It's the kind of seam they use in denim levis.)

For a large tote bag, the main panels should measure about 16″ x 20″ plus margins—I suggest using a strip pattern, as shown.

1. Piece main panels and side panels and cut a bottom panel 8″ x 20″—no margins. Cut linings and battings to match.

2. Cut two strips for handles 20″ long and 4¾″ wide. Fold lengthwise, right sides together,

454.

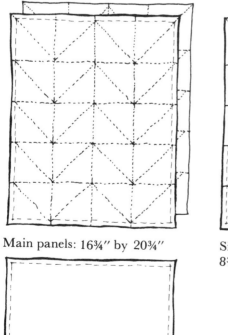

Main panels: 16¾″ by 20¾″

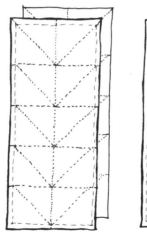

Side panels:
8¾″ by 20¾″

Handle:
20″ by 4¾″

Bottom panel: 16¾″ by 8¾″

and sew the long side with a ⅜″ seam. Turn right side out and press, having the seam in the middle of the underside. Cut two strips of batting 20″ x 2¾″ and insert them into the handles, using a knitting needle or a crochet hook.

3. Assemble the two main panels as described for the smaller bag. First lay out the batting, then the patchwork top, right side up. Baste handles in place, as shown, with the seamless side against the right side of the work; with the seamless side against the right side of the work; let the ends of the handles extend above the upper edge of the patch-work, about ½″. Lay the lining over all, right side down, and stitch across the upper edge from edge to edge, joining in handles.

455. Top (and batting)   Lining

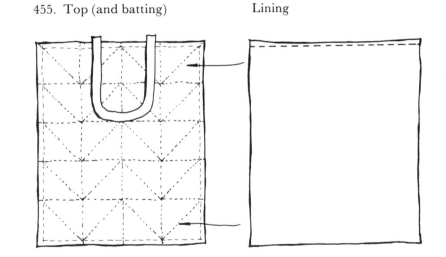

4. Turn the work right side out. For extra strength, top-stitch across the enclosed handle ends, as shown. Stitch again ⅛″ below that. Make these lines of stitching extra strong, for they will be supporting the full weight of whatever is in the bag.

5. Assemble the side panels, batting first, then top and lining, right sides together. Stitch across the upper edge from edge to edge. Turn right side out.

456. Lining top (and batting)

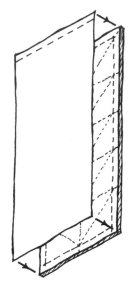

457. Trim ⅜″ margin

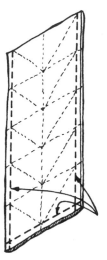

458. Pocket inside

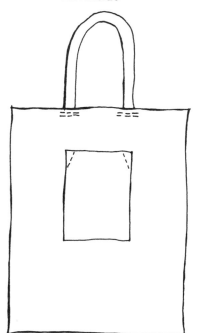

6. Assemble the bottom panel in the usual way, lining-batting-top, and quilt all pieces by hand or machine all the way to the edge if desired. Trim away the ⅜″ seam margins from all edges of the four side panels.

7. For a pocket for wallet and keys and so on, cut a piece of fabric 8½″ x 6 ½″. Turn in and press ¼″ hem all around. Stitch hem in place across the upper edge. Baste the pocket to the inside of one panel, as shown, having the top about 4″ below the upper edge of bag; this makes it virtually inaccessible to pickpockets. Hem it strongly in place, and reinforce the stitching at the upper edge, for this area takes a lot of strain as you plunge your hand in and out trying to find keys. Either take a few strong tacks, or use about an inch of machine top-stitching on each side, as shown. This shows on the front, of course, but not as much as you might suppose.

For strength, the panels of this bag are seamed with bias tape, which you buy ready to use (I recommend it) or make yourself. To make it, cut 1″ wide bias strips and turn in and press ¼″ margins

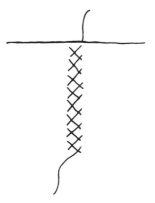

on either side. To buy, look for hemmed tape with a finished width of ½″ or more. It comes in all colors and it's stronger than anything.

You will need 8 strips of tape 20¾″ long, and two strips 56¾″ long—you will have to piece them, of course.

1. To assemble, lay two side panels edge to edge, as shown. Catch-stitch them together or secure them with a long, wide machine zigzag stitch.

2. Take two of the bias strips 20¾″ long; turn under and press a ⅜″ hem at upper edge of each tape. Center one strip over the seam, with the hemmed end of the tape at the finished edge of the panels, and baste. Turn the work over and similarly baste the other tape in place through all layers on either side of the seam, as shown. This will be difficult; you may need to use the zipper foot that is hinged to ride more easily over many layers, and use a size 16 needle. Repeat until all four seams are completed.

3. Set the bottom panel in place and catch-stitch or zigzag to hold. Turn in and press ⅜″ hems on each end of the remaining two tapes. Baste the tapes in place inside and outside the seams and sew them down with two continuous lines of stitching around four sides of the bottom. You will probably have to turn the wheel by hand to get through the worst clumps of seam margins, and at those moments I find it also helps to swear loudly. Rest assured that it is worth the trouble; for 20 minutes of annoyance you get years of use and pleasure from this bag. And once you have the habit of carrying it you'll realize how vastly annoying, wasteful, and inconvenient are your daily rounds without it.

PROJECTS FOR YOU TO WORK OUT

If you have thought through the described procedures for these projects, even if you haven't actually made any of them, you now know all the basic techniques for making practically anything

460. Strips basted over seams inside and out

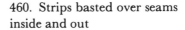

461. Seam strips top-stitched in place

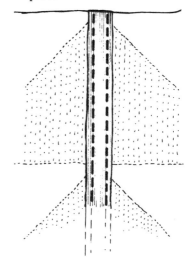

that can be sewn in either patchwork or quilting or both. You know that:

a. Unquilted patchwork must be lined to avoid unraveling seam margins.

b. To make a seam between quilted fabrics that will be finished on both sides, you sew the top layers as usual, right sides together, and on the inside you turn in the seam margins of the lining pieces and slip-stitch them together.

c. To make a very strong seam between quilted pieces, finished on both sides, you cover and reinforce the seam on both sides with hemmed stripping and stitch down either side of the seam through all layers of quilted stuff and stripping.

462. A tea cosy

Here then is a list of suggestions for projects you might work out in quilting or patchwork.

A Tea Cosy: absolutely *de rigueur* for British quilters. Just quilt two dome-shaped panels large enough to cover your tea pot, and join them according to plan b.

A Coffee Pot Cosy: a quilted cylinder with a top on it keeps the pot nice and warm as you lounge around the dinner table waiting for the chocolate soufflé to rise.

A TV Cosy: it wouldn't have to be quilted, unless your set is subject to colds, but a lined patchwork hood for the television would surely be nicer to look at than that gray blind eye.

Patchwork covers can be made for anything you consider unsightly. A small cylinder with a top can cover the extra roll of toilet paper perched on top of the tank, or a larger cylinder with a bottom might cover empty coffee cans—either the one you keep by the stove for bacon drippings or ones you give away filled with Christmas cookies or homemade Granola.

Aprons: made of patchwork and lined with muslin.

Patchwork Pockets: lined and sewn to an apron you already have, or any garment that needs a pocket.

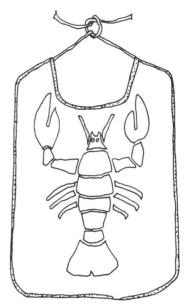

463. A lobster bib

A Quilted Jacket: for a child or a slim adult. Choose a pattern with a minimum of pockets and darts; one with a Nehru collar would have an appropriately mandarin look.

Bibs: for a baby, a patchwork bib lined with softest vinyl. For adults, a large lobster bib made of terrycloth with an appliqué, either a literal lobster or an abstract shape suggesting one. This is a great gift for people who live or summer by the sea and who generally clutter up the environment with disposable paper lobster bibs after their shore dinners.

Appliqué bibs lined with soft vinyl are nice for babies too. The best one I've seen was made by Marcia Schonzeit—a brown velour bib with a picture of a fried egg on it.

Floor Furniture: enormous cubes and pillows are nice to sit on around a fire or in any informal room where most of the proceedings are at ground level. Just follow the instructions for a knife-edge pillow, but make the panels much bigger—30″ square or more. Stuff the pillow with foam chips, kapok, or quilt batting. For variation, sew a large leather or wooden button tightly through all layers in the exact center of the pillow.

Mountain Artisans, a sewing cooperative in West Virginia, also offers a piece of floor furniture in the shape of an enormous foam cube with patchwork. Essentially this is the same thing as the baby blocks (page 109), but it measures about two feet on a side.

Puffed Patchwork: patchwork pillows and bedspreads made of rows of puffed-up squares of different color fabrics have become very popular in the last year or two; I confess to a certain prejudice against them, not because they aren't clever—they are, very clever—but because I don't think they're patchwork. The whole point of patchwork design is to make all the separate pieces work together to create some graphic effect, however simple. If you puff up each piece so that it stands completely apart from all the adjoining ones, you end up with a series of discrete, unrelated squares, not patch-work.

However, pre-stuffing is a very useful technique, particularly if you want a very warm fluffy comforter and don't want to tuft or quilt. Perhaps rather than using it to mock patchwork, you can devise some other kind of design for it that will take advantage of its special qualities.

Basically, a puffed unit is made up of two squares (or triangles or rectangles) having the top piece two or three inches larger than the lining. For a little pillow top made of puffed squares, you would cut lining squares of muslin 3″ square and top pieces of patterned fabric 4½″ square. For the squares of a comforter, the lining squares would be 8″ and the top pieces 10″ or more. (Cut a sample or two to see how much puff you want in the top.)

Baste the top square to the bottom square on three sides, wrong sides together, so that the edges and corners match, as shown. Stuff the piece with dacron batting, and baste the fourth side in place. In this fashion baste and stuff as many squares as you need to make up the top of the pillow or comforter. Then sew them together as you would any piece of patchwork. Place two squares puffed sides together; stitch with a sewing machine, taking a ¼″ or ⅜″ seam. Join the squares into horizontal rows, then join the rows together with long seams, taking care to match the seams between the squares. Remove the basting thread.

To press, set the iron on warm (the lower end of Permanent Press) and go over the seams with the tip of the iron. You can do this on the front or the back. Just be sure not to iron down any of the puffing, because it will ruin the effect you have just created, and because direct high heat melts dacron.

For a Comforter, make a lining the size of the top and center it over the top, right sides together. Stitch around three sides and halfway up the fourth, taking a ¼″ to ½″ seam. Turn the piece right side out, and slip-stitch the last part of the

464. Square of puffed patch-work

236

seam closed. To prevent the layers from shifting, add tacks or tufts, two or three in each row, evenly spaced along the seam lines.

For a Pillow, cut a backing piece the same size as the top; sew top and backing right sides together around three sides, turn right side out, and stuff with dacron batting or a pre-cut pillow form. Slip-stitch the last side closed.

Chair Backs: quilted patchwork makes a handsome padding for the backs of ladderback chairs. Make a panel of quilted patchwork in a rectangle the size of the chair back, attach the panel to the chair with ribbons or tapes sewn onto the top corners of the piece and tie to the top of the chair.

Patchwork Hoods for Kitchen Appliances: make rectangular hoods for toasters, cylinders for electric blenders, mixers, or juicers.

Collars and Cuffs: when the collars and cuffs of a favorite garment become frayed, cut them off the garment and use them for the patterns to make new ones of patchwork.

Purses: in needlework and craft shops you can buy wooden or metal frames with which to make evening bags; they often come in kits with instructions for cutting and decorating the fabric body of the purse; you can use the patterns to cut your own and decorate with patchwork or fancy quilting.

Roll-Up Traveling Jewelry Case: a quilted rectangle about 12" x 18". Make the outside of satin, or cotton sateen if you want the piece washable; the inside is of muslin or soft, patterned cotton. On the inside, blind-hem pockets for necklaces and bracelets, and smaller ones for earrings. Leave part of the lining empty for pinning brooches directly to the fabric. On the outside sew two cotton, satin, or grosgrain ribbons to the exact middle of the rectangle. Roll the case into a cylinder for traveling and secure the roll with the ribbons.

Traveling Sewing Case: make the same way as

465. Quilted chairback

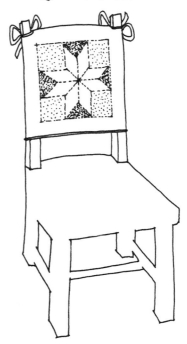

466. Jewelry case, inside

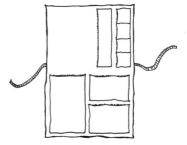

467. Jewelry or sewing kit, rolled and tied

468. Glove case, inside

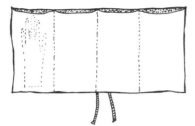

469. Glove case, folded

470. Tea cosy doll

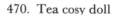

the jewelry case, but make pockets to fit small spools of thread, scissors, and so on. Use the blank spaces for a row of pins and needles in assorted sizes.

A Glove Case: for traveling, make a rectangle of quilted fabric 10″ x 20″; hem four rectangular pockets to the inside, each 5″ x 10″. On the outside, sew ribbons at the exact center of the case; slip a pair of gloves into each pocket and fold the two outside pockets toward the center, then fold again in half. Tie the case closed with the ribbons.

Make other traveling cases, for stockings, cosmetics, underwear, and so on. Just make a square or rectangular pouch with a fold-over cuff to close it. (See directions for Comforter Cover.)

Also, consider quilted slippers or scuffs for traveling, and quilted covers for things with sharp edges like scissors and letter openers.

Eye Glasses Case—quilted to protect the lenses from jars and jolts.

Cigarette Case—with an outside pocket for matches or a lighter.

Stuffed Animals: you can get patterns for animals and dolls at notions stores; most pattern companies include a section of such sewing projects at the back of the pattern book. Cut each section—the tail, each leg, the body, each ear, and so on—from a different fabric.

Dolls—remember the Patchwork Girl of Oz? She was made entirely of crazy-pieced scraps, with two button eyes and two strands of yarn for hair. Make or buy a pattern for a cloth doll, and build the pieces out of tiny, irregular scraps.

Tea Cosy Dolls: if memory serves, my mother (or grandmother) had a doll with a wide, quilted hoop skirt that doubled as a tea cosy. It was quite a sensation to see a doll come waltzing in on the tea tray with a tea pot concealed among her unmentionables.

The doll has no legs and the skirt should be stiffened with an interlining like buckram, so that it stands by itself; machine-quilting will be best in this case.

Reversible Mammy Doll: when I was a tad they made reversible dolls very much like the tea cosy doll, except that underneath the long, stiff skirt instead of a tea pot there was another doll upside down. A patchwork skirt would be ideal for such a doll, since patchwork must be fully lined and thus reversible anyway.

Frames for Pictures and Mirrors: buy a cheap frame at the dime store and cover it with patchwork or quilted fabric attached to the frame with contact cement—Elmer's or Weldwood.

Frame a Patchwork Block—either a complicated one of your own making, or one cut from an old quilt.

SALVAGING OLD QUILTS

Sometimes you can find old quilts that are too ratty to save but which nevertheless have some blocks still completely intact. There are lots of things to do with these in addition to framing; using them for pillow tops comes to mind as most obvious, but if you can pick up a couple with large usable areas (badly damaged quilts should be inexpensive, no matter how beautiful they are) you can even cover chairs and sofas with them. If you can salvage a long rectangular section, use it for a runner on a mantelpiece or the top of an upright piano; or upholster the top of a piano bench or stool.

Lamp Shades: patchwork lined with white muslin stretched on the wire frame of an old lampshade gives a beautiful stained glass effect with the light shining through it.

Table Cloths: patchwork lined with muslin can cover a dining or end table. For dining, you can also make matching patchwork napkins and napkin rings.

Shawls: for evening, make a shawl of crazy-pieced silks and velvets, lined with silk or satin.

471. Tree hangings

472. Quilted knee patch

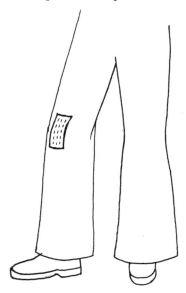

Pajama Case: a small patchwork pillow case lined with muslin and closed on one side with a zipper, can contain pajamas and nightgowns during the day and serve as a throw pillow on the made-up bed.

Apartment Attics: for storage space in a crowded aparment, you can buy large, sturdy cardboard boxes at dime stores and cover them with sheets of patchwork, anchored with contact cement or white glue. (After you apply the glue, tape the area in place with masking tape and leave it alone until the glue has dried, at least overnight.)

Little Stuffed Lumps and Beasties for Christmas Tree Decorations: sew ribbons to their little heads for hanging and decorate with sequins and spangles or anything else that appeals to you.

Wall Hangings: sew loops to the top of the piece to be hung; slip a dowel through the loops and attach a length of picture wire to it; hang it as you would a picture. (A dowel is a round stick; a broomstick is a dowel and so is a pencil. Sometimes you can get them in hardware stores; if not, go to a lumberyard. Look in the Yellow Pages under Lumber—they're everywhere.)

If the piece you are hanging needs a little tension to make it hang smooth and straight, you can attach a second row of loops to the bottom and put a dowel through them to weigh it down. Or, consider stretching the whole thing on wooden stretchers as a painter does canvas. Ask about stretchers, and how to use them, at an art supply store.

Curtains: patchwork lined with muslin does a lot to dress up a window and looks lovely with the sun behind it. Measure the height and width of the window, then piece two panels of patchwork as long as the window and three-quarters as wide; curtains hang most gracefully if their combined span is half again the width of the window. Line each curtain with white muslin, and attach cloth loops along the top, evenly spaced about four or five inches apart. Hang the curtains on the cage rods.

If you want the curtains to really block the light, for example, in a child's room at nap-time, they can be filled and quilted as well.

Patches: A final tip, returning the ennobled patch to whence it came. When patching a garment in a very frayed place or in an area that bears a lot of strain, try quilting the patch for extra strength. Use batting or not, depending on where the patch is and how thick the fabric is to be sewn through.

11 MISCELLANEOUS INFORMATION: CARING FOR QUILTS; QUILTMAKING FOR MONEY

CARING FOR QUILTS

Washing a quilt lined with cotton batting is a matter requiring some care and skill. Waterlogged cotton batting swells and grows extremely heavy, and the weight and strain could break the quilting stitches if they were not very small and strong and even. A quilt must never be twisted or wrung, for that too might break the quilting, yet the cotton cannot be allowed to remain damp too long because it might mildew. Quilts used to be washed gently by hand in large tubs on hot summer days, then hung in the sun to dry.

Quilts filled with dacron batting may be washed by hand or machine in warm water. They can be dried on the line, but they come out smoothest and fluffiest if tumble-dried in a machine. *Never* iron a quilt; it ruins the effect of the quilting. If you want to, you can use one of those steam-pressing gadgets that steam out wrinkles without touching the fabric.

Quilts that are stored most of the time, and don't really need washing, should still be aired in the sun once a year to avoid yellowing and prevent mildew. They should be washed every five years, dirty or not, to keep the colors fresh.

Very large quilts should not be washed in a home washing machine, because if they are jammed too tightly into the tub they will probably not get clean, and they will certainly not get rinsed thoroughly; deposits of soap or detergent will make the quilt grey or yellow. If you are quite sure your king- or queen-sized quilt has enough quilting or knots or tacks to be washed safely, you can take it to a laundromat that has big industrial machines. Otherwise, have it dry-cleaned. A quilt made with velvet or silk should always be dry-cleaned, as should a quilt made with fabrics that may shrink or run. Such quilts should be cleaned as little as possible, because the chemicals used in dry-cleaning are harsh, and sooner or later the strain will tell on the seams or fabrics. (Remember that a well-made quilt should last a lot longer than an average piece of clothing.)

If you have an old quilt that you value, avoid having it cleaned in any way, but if it becomes really necessary, try to locate a cleaner specializing in the care and preservation of old or precious fabrics. If you can't find one, call a museum that displays antique clothing or furniture and ask them who cares for their things and how it is done.

MAKING MONEY MAKING QUILTS

Well-designed, handmade quilts offer such an unusual combination of beauty and genuine usefulness that it seems there should be money in them somewhere. After all, people pay hundreds of dollars for prints and lithographs, which are not one of a kind and they can't even sleep under them, and they sometimes pay hundreds of dollars for machine-made bedspreads, which are neither art nor Art. However, it probably won't come as a surprise to hear that making a living making quilts, or doing anything by hand in competition with mass production, is at best a risky proposition.

For one thing, no matter how beautiful or unusual the item, there is a definite limit to what people will spend to cover a bed. The modern maker of handmade quilts is competing, on the one hand, with factories which produce faster and cheaper than a single craftsman no matter what the product. On the other, he/she is competing with a lot of dead people; the market is flooded with beautiful and well-preserved quilts that took hundreds of hours to make and cost from $35 to $85. No matter how many short cuts you take, if you try to compete with the available supply of traditional quilts, you end up working for 17¢ an hour.

The obvious alternative to this is to try to market the quilts as Art, since there is no limit to what people will pay for something to hang on the wall. Here, oddly enough, the very usefulness of the quilt works against you. The fact that they could conceivably keep warm under the thing at night seems to convince people that it is not Art, but a bedspread temporarily hung on a wall.

SELLING TO DEPARTMENT STORES

If you try to market your quilts through department stores, the first problem you encounter is that the store will have to take a 100% mark-up in order to pay their overhead and make a profit. That means if you need to get $30 for a baby quilt in order to pay yourself for your time and expenses, they have to sell if for $60, and very few people will pay that much for a baby quilt even if it shows an exact rendering of the Mona Lisa. The second problem is that if the item is a success, they will probably want you to provide them with 12 dozen more by next Tuesday—it just isn't any use to them to get one every three weeks. There are exceptions to this: some department stores have small specialty boutiques which might like to handle handmade items; you might even work something out with a regular bedspread department, so give it a try if you want to. Prowl around the store looking for a department that might be most interested in your work, then go home and call for an appointment with the buyer for that department. Take her an example of your work and be prepared to tell her exactly how much you want for each piece and how fast you can produce them.

BOUTIQUES

Some people have some luck selling through small shops and boutiques. Boutiques will be happy to take one item at a time, but most small operations take things on consignment rather than buying them outright. That means they take 40% and give you 60% *if* they sell, which is a better percentage than when you sell to a big store, but if they don't sell it you get nothing (except the quilt back). Also, a small store has limited display space. If the quilt is a large and spectacular design that must be seen in toto to be appreciated, you're out of luck; the quilt will almost surely be displayed folded or artfully draped so that the customer sees a corner of the pattern. If you find a boutique that is interested in handmade items, and in you, concentrate on small items, like baby quilts and household objects such as you find in the projects chapter here. Be sure you get receipts for everything you give them and agree on *their* asking price, of which you get 60 percent, ahead of time. Don't let them put you in the position of naming the price you will accept for the item, because if they think it is too low, they can sell it for much more and still only give you what you asked for.

GALLERIES

If spectacular graphic design in patchwork is your thing, you can try to find an art gallery to handle your work. A gallery is the only place with the space to display large quilts as they should be seen, but most gallery directors hold to a sharp dichotomy between Arts and Crafts; they may buy one of your pieces to put on their own bed at home, but the chances are they won't hang them. Some galleries, especially in resort and rural areas, are loosening up about crafts, or Folk Arts as they are more likely to call them, and some galleries even devote themselves exclusively to folk arts. If you can locate such a place, or want to try the rounds of the regular art galleries, carry with you a portfolio of *good* photographs of your work, and at least one small quilt in person so that they can touch and feel, and gauge the skill of workmanship. If you do suceed in interesting a gallery, payment will either be on a 40 percent for them, 60 percent for you basis, or a 50/50 split, and you get paid only for the pieces that are sold. The rest you get back, of course. You and the director will probably decide together what the market will bear in the way of prices, but be prepared to name the lowest price you can afford to accept, and stick by it.

DISPLAYING YOUR OWN WORK

If you yourself have adequate display space in your home or studio, you can try staging your own show. Put ads in local newspapers and magazines, post notices at supermarkets and other community gathering places. You could advertise one show at a specific time and place (Sunday afternoons are best) and welcome all comers, or you could advertise yourself as a gallery that opens by appointment only. If you do the latter it is best to include a price range in the advertisement (say something like "Prices begin at $75"), so that people will be aware that you are not opening your home to them for your health. It is also most comfortable to have the prices marked on the items. It may embarrass people to have to ask you what things cost, and it may embarrass you to tell them. At heart, most Americans don't enjoy bargaining, but if you find one that does, he/she will be just as willing to bargain about a price on a tag as one that you quote out of the air.

CRAFT FAIRS

During the summer months, many areas have craft fairs and sidewalk art shows where artists and craftsmen come to display their work. Some people work all winter on a collection, then spend the summer making the rounds of the fairs selling their work and taking orders for the coming winter. The one at Bennington, Vermont, is the biggest in the Northeast, but there are others all over the country. The big ones attract not only tourists and private collectors, but also buyers from shops and stores who come to place wholesale orders. Generally, you pay a small fee for a booth and display and sell your work yourself, but some shows ask you to send the pieces for them to display and sell. Some shows are juried—you have to submit photographs and samples to a panel to get permission to exhibit; others are first come, first served.

If you want to learn where and how to exhibit, the American Crafts Council publishes a magazine called *Craft Horizons* which will keep you informed about regional craft events and competitive exhibitions all over the country. A subscribing membership entitles you to the magazine and free admission to the Museum of Contemporary Crafts in New York. For information about their programs and memberships, write to:

American Crafts Council
44 W. 53rd Street
New York, N. Y. 10019

SELLING THROUGH DECORATORS

An ideal way to work, for anyone interested in doing large, elaborate quilts, is to have each piece commissioned before it is made. That way you can afford to put in as much time and care as you want because you know ahead of time what you will be paid. An interior decorator, planning a room for a client, could come to you with a particular problem—a wall hanging, matching spreads for twin beds, a king-size quilt, and so on. He/she tells you as much as possible about the client's tastes and perhaps shows you swatches of fabrics being used in the room for curtains, upholstery, and carpeting. You then draw up one or two designs and submit them with swatches of the fabrics you think will look best, and you and the decorator decide on a fair price for the work. The decorator then submits the proposal to the client, and if all agree, you provide quilts made in the size and colors the decorator requires.

One snag in this procedure is that unlike most of the decorator's sources, you do not keep a line of fabrics on hand; you probably buy retail, and if the client takes too long making up his/her mind, you may find that the fabrics you submitted are all out of stock. If you take a chance and buy the fabrics before the client approves the job, you may be stuck with them. Still, if it is a major job, you are probably only gambling ten or fiteen dollars against the chance of making a hundred or two; and you must be prepared to take risks if you are in business for yourself.

A greater problem is the matter of getting yourself listed with decorators in the first place. The best way is to pull strings; if you or your friends know any decorators, or anybody connected with the field of interior design, pump them for names of decorators who work on private homes and might be interested in custom design and handmade things. Call the decorators and explain what you do; ask if you may bring samples and photographs to show them; be prepared to quote approximate prices and to estimate the amount of time you need to complete a project of a given size and complexity. The price you quote is the price you expect to get. The decorator's cut or fee is between him/her and the client. Be prepared to work for a little less than you might otherwise, because you are theoretically selling wholesale at this point.

If you don't have a private way of getting names of decorators to talk to, look in the Yellow Pages under Interior Decoration and Design. If you have the nerve, just start calling decorators and firms, explain what you do, and ask if they are sufficiently interested to look at your work. It might be a little embarrassing, but all you need is one or two decorators who really like what you do to keep yourself in business.

QUILTING FOR MONEY

In another age there were women who quilted at home on other people's quilts for pocket money, and groups which quilted other people's quilts for money to give to charity. Now these women are hard to find, but there are more and more people making patchwork who haven't time to quilt properly and who would rather send the work out to be quilted by hand than by machine. If you want to work at home and would like to take in quilting, there are several ways you might go about it.

First, advertise in local papers and magazines. Second, write to Stearns and Foster and see what you have to do to get on their list of professional quilters. Third, go to any stores and shops in your area that sell old or new handmade quilts and ask if they have any work for you quilting new quilts or repairing old ones; if they do not, ask permission to post a little sign with your name and address and the message that you want to do quilting. People who have made a quilt top that they want finished, or who discover an old one made by their grandmother which was never quilted, generally turn first to stores which sell quilts as the likeliest source of lore and information. And in general they are right, for people who collect, handle, and resell quilts tend to absorb a fund of information about quilts and their makers. In New York, outstanding quilt places are America Hurrah, which has a fantastic collection of old quilts for sale, and the Gazebo, a flower shop with a big room in back devoted to old and new quilts and the New York branch of Mountain Artisans upstairs. If you are over 60, you have a perfect hang-out and outlet in The Elder Craftsman in New York. Across the country Women's Exchanges take in handwork of all kinds on consignment, and they are also more likely to be interested in you if you don't look too young and/or prosperous.

If you undertake to finish someone's quilt, the owner provides the top, the backing and binding material, and batting; he/she may want to decide on a quilting pattern, or it may be left to you. You supply the thread and the skill. Decide on your charge for the work beforehand; old-time quilters used to work for something like a dollar a spool, which is insane. You could charge either by the spool or the hour—$2.25 to $3.00 per hour is about the going rate for other kinds of hand-sewing.

QUILTING COOPERATIVES

At present there are two quilt cooperatives that seem to be making a go of things on a nation-wide scale; the oldest and best known is Mountain Artisans, whose national headquarters is in Charleston, West Virginia. They have a house artist who does all the quilt and clothing designs and chooses fabrics for each; the pieces are pre-cut on industrial machines at the main office, then distributed for sewing to the 150 women who belong to the co-op. The women work at home for a guaranteed price per hour and the goods are promoted and distributed in various market areas around the country. The overhead for such an operation is huge and the first years were very rough going; there were times when nothing sold and no one got paid, but the groups held together and Mountain Artisans is now probably the most successful such operation in the country. The fashion industry has honored them with a special award for the excellence of the clothing they offer, and the quilt designs get better every year.

The prices for Mountain Artisan products are sky-high; they have to be, in order to guarantee the women a decent hourly wage and to promote the pieces adequately. Their customers consider the prices worth it, because successful promotion has made them aware that the money goes not to a profit-taking corporation, but to women who are extremely good at what they do but who had no dignified way to make it pay before Mountain Artisans helped them to organize.

The other co-op that is doing business nationwide is the Dakotah Handcrafts group, which sell its work through department stores. (Mountain Artisans sells clothes in retail stores, but the quilts and other large items are sold wholesale through decorators.) The Dakotah group makes a set number of quilt and pillow designs, which can be ordered in various colors and sizes; the designs are mostly original, based on Indian motifs, and machine-pieced or appliquéd, then hand-quilted. The departments stores display the quilts, take the orders and take their cut, and about 600 women, 350 working full time, make the quilts to fill the orders. The group was organized with the help of Vista and a professional marketing consultant from New York, after an attempt to attract outside industry to their economically depressed area of South Dakota failed. About two-thirds of the women are Sioux Indians, but 200 are white, and the project represents the first time the two have worked together in this region. While the Mountain Artisans work in their homes, the Dakotah women gather in central areas to sew and work around quilting frames; for many, the traveling means hitchhiking or walking long distances in one of the severest climates in the country—temperatures range from over 100° in summer to −30° in winter.

A third group, the Martin Luther King Freedom Quilting Bee, seems to have fallen victim to the difficulties of marketing and promotion and competing with the flood of inexpensive antique quilts on the market. The Quilting Bee was composed of black women in Alabama who made contemporary puff coverlets and extremely beautiful traditional quilts in unusual fabrics, such as richly colored velveteen with several cotton prints in related shades. Unlike the other two cooperatives, the women of the Quilting Bee apparently designed their own quilts instead of working with a professional, and the quality of the design was outstanding. Also, unlike the other two, the Quilting Bee did both piecework and quilting by hand. The women were evidently working on speculation—in other words, they were not paid until after the quilts were sold. Given the time and overhead involved, it is no wonder that they were unable to make a profit, but it is certainly a loss, both to them and to us.

It is a luxury, both emotionally and economically, to be able to work purely for your own satisfaction. In our society, being paid a decent wage for what you do is a sign of your dignity and personhood. Children are petted and praised and thanked in gushing tones; full-fleged adults are paid in the true coin of our respect: money. Some of us can afford to forego money, but we all need respect. People tired of everything machine-made are getting more and more interested in the craftsman and the artisan, and yet one senses that it is still slightly ridiculous to try to make a living with your hands, as if you wouldn't do it if you could possibly do something else that paid better. For those of us who already have all the money and respect we need, let us thank our stars, and for those of us who do not, let us hope a day is coming when the work of the serious craftsman/woman will be as well respected in the marketplace as the work of the serious plumber.

12 MAIL-ORDER SOURCES OF GOODS AND SERVICES

Vermont Country Store
Weston, Vermont 05161

Calico: The Vermont Country Store carries a line of the real thing in eighteen prints and colors. For 50¢ they will send you swatches, plus their catalogue of everything from poke bonnets to oil lamps, a treasure in itself.

Stearns & Foster Company
Quilting Department
Cincinnati, Ohio 45215

Batting, Piecework, and Appliqué Patterns, Quilting Patterns, Quilting Frame Blueprint, Hand-Quilters: Stearns & Foster make a line of battings which are available in some department stores, and by mail order. It comes in sizes 90″ x 108″ or 81″ x 96″ in dacron, 81″ x 108″ and 45″ x 60″ (for a crib) in cotton. Their traditional patchwork and quilting patterns are beautiful, if demanding. To order any of these products, write to the Quilting Department and they will promptly return to you catalogues and price lists with instructions for ordering the item you want. They also keep a list of people around the country who do hand-quilting.

Sears Roebuck Company
(Look in the phone book for the address of the outlet nearest you.)

Quilt Batting, Comfortor Batting, Quilting Frames: Descriptions and prices (which vary from time to time) are listed in their catalogue, which you obtain by contacting the outlet in your area. All products are first rate and the list prices are slightly less than you will find anywhere else. However, shipping and delivery charges vary according to the weight of the item and the distance it must be shipped, so ask about these charges before you order.

H. Houst & Sons
Woodstock, New York 12498

Quilting Thread: Houst carries Coats & Clark silicone-coated quilting thread in a variety of colors. They will send you a box of six spools for $2.84 plus postage, but write to them before you send money because it's a hot item, difficult to locate elsewhere, and they, like the rest of us, have occasional difficulty getting and keeping it in stock.

J. Schacter Corp.
115 Allen St.
New York, New York 10002

Quilt and Comforter Battings, Down Filling, Machine Quilting: Schacter's will stuff your hand-made quilt with dacron or down and machine-quilt it for you. Write or call them for shipping charges and prices.

13 RECOMMENDED READING

There are a number of interesting, if dated, books on quilts available in libraries; many are worth skimming. You should also watch for the extraordinary collection of pieced quilts owned by Jonathan Holstein and Gail van de Hoof in case it makes a visit to your neighborhood. It has been exhibited at the Whitney Museum in New York, in Paris, and at the Renwick Gallery of the National Gallery of Fine Arts in Washington. A catalogue of the Renwick exhibit was put out by the Smithsonian Institution's Traveling Exhibition Service; you may be able to get a copy by writing the Smithsonian in Washington.

The Shelburne Museum also puts out an excellent catalogue of outstanding pieces in its collection; the title is *Pieced Work and Appliqué Quilts at Shelburne Museum*, by Lillian Baker Carlisle. It contains 99 black and white photographs, and running commentary. To order, write to the Shelburne Museum, Shelburne, Vermont 05482. You should enclose your name and address and a check or money order for $4.00 plus 25¢ for postage.

If you want to go the whole hog, the ultimate source book in the field is *America's Quilts and Coverlets* by Safford and Bishop, published by E. P. Dutton & Company, Inc., 1972. It is a beautiful book with both color plates and black and white photographs, covering piecework and appliqué quilts and numerous other kinds of coverlets as well. It costs $25.00; if it's not available at a bookstore near you, you can order it from the publisher at 201 Park Avenue South, New York, N. Y. 10003.

INDEX